A COURAGEOUS WALK

THROUGH LIFE

A Courageous Walk through Life

The Story of AUNT FANNIE

Jeannine W. Hamburg
as told by Edward Hamburg

A Courageous Walk Through Life: The Story of Aunt Fannie

Copyright © Jeannine W. Hamburg 1995

Published by Myrte Press
1216 Crane Drive
Cherry Hill, NJ 08003

Publisher's Cataloging in Publication
(Prepared by Quality Books Inc.)

Hamburg, Jeannine W.
  A courageous walk through life : the story of Aunt Fannie / Jeannine W. Hamburg. -- 1 st ed.
  p. cm.
  Preassigned LCCN: 95-94355
  ISBN 0-9623501-1-7 (pbk)
  ISBN 0-9623501-2-5 (hc)

  1. Shulitzky, Fannie. 2.Immigrants--United States--Biography. 3. Poliomyelitis--Patients--Biography. I. Title.

CT275.S5855H35 1995   304.8'73'04771
                    QBI95-20249

Cover Design: Susan Weiss

Manufactured in the United States of America
First Edition

To Myrte and Isaac

To your long life

ACKNOWLEDGMENTS

Thanks to my family who encouraged me to write this book. They were the catalyst of my convictions. My loving husband Edward encouraged me when I needed it the most and who, during his recollections was surprised at how much he remembered from the past. My son Jeff had the foresight to tape some of Aunt Fannie's stories while she was alive. He and his wife Leonore prodded me on until the finished product was in view. They read through my first rough manuscripts and made historical corrections. Karen, my daughter, acted as an advisor throughout the whole process.

My gratitude extends to Rosalie and Milton Alson, Rabbi Samuel and Evelyn Berkowitz, Paul and Phyllis Brown, Sarah Dick and Joseph Hamburg who made significant contributions. Jean Fogel, Clare Leonard, and Ruth Weiss offered valuable suggestions for changes in the manuscript.

Nancy Morse Kelly gave me direction in my first writings and Linda DeFelice at Gloucester County College was ready and willing to answer my questions, and always seemed to have the right answers. Tony Butler converted the disks when I updated my computer.

I learned from Gloria Delamar who excelled in the editing of the final manuscript, and from Susan Weiss who typeset the manuscript and designed the cover of the book. Tina Edginton and Heather Weisman saw me through to publication.

There are many other people, too numerous to mention, who helped me in various ways. I appreciate their invaluable assistance.

It is through the efforts of all of these caring people that the story of Aunt Fannie will become a legend.

CONTENTS

A COURAGEOUS WALK
THROUGH LIFE

INTRODUCTION

It was through my parents that I first became acquainted with Aunt Fannie. Their association with the Shulitzky family began many years prior to my marriage to Fannie's nephew, Edward—before he and I were born. My mother and Fannie's elder sister Gertie had been friends in Russia dating back to the early 1900's. Their friendship continued following their emigration to America, where each of their families had settled in Philadelphia.

After their marriage, my parents often were the guests of the Shulitzky family on Sundays when it was customary for families to gather together at the end of the week. When Gertie married, she and her husband spent their honeymoon at my parent's house in a small town in New Jersey. My father convinced his friends Gertie and Thomas to settle in the same town in which he operated a business.

During the time I was growing up I was aware of Fannie's presence, but I did not know her really well. As destiny would have it, Edward and I fell in love and married. Edward's Aunt Fannie became my aunt, also. After our marriage, it didn't take long for me to realize that Aunt Fannie was a very special person. I came to admire her attitude toward life, and her courage.

Toward the end of Aunt Fannie's life I was searching for ideas for a next book. One day as Edward and I were listening to the fascinating recounts of her history, the conception came within my grasp. The chronicle of her life, which is narrated by Edward, was waiting be told.

PROLOGUE

Memories tugged at my heart as I walked up the steep incline of steps to a rowhouse in West Philadelphia. When I set foot onto the cemented porch leading to my aunt's comfortable, but modest apartment and turned the key to unlock the door, my thoughts traced the path of my heritage, and my mind leaped to the last living member of my family, Aunt Fannie.

It was a sultry day in August of 1990 that I came to search through my dear aunt's mementos and personal belongings—to break up house—the comforts with which Fannie wished to remain until her dying day. But wishes do not always come true.

My mother's sister, Fannie, lived here with my grandmother, Bubba as we called her, until Bubba died thirty-two years before. I envisioned the happy times I had spent in this house with my family. I could still smell the pungent odors of my grandmother's cooking when on Sunday afternoons my parents, aunts, uncles and cousins gathered here to discuss the important issues of the week—and events that were not so important—as well.

The front door of Aunt Fannie's apartment opened into the living room where white plaster had fallen from the ceiling into a defined pattern onto the green rug, thinned by the scuffing of my aunt's shoes. I could visualize my aunt moving about in the apartment with her characteristic walk, the heel of the lame left leg supporting her body as she thrusts the strong leg forward.

I studied the variegated plant sitting on the dusty coffee

1

table, withered and brown. My eyes then gazed upon the faded oblong and oval shapes of the carved frames that once covered the walls; frames that held pictures of my grandparents, long deceased, aunts and uncles, and those of my parents. I mentally captured relative's faces whose eyes seemingly reflected a multiplicity of personalities. On the mantle of the pseudo fireplace rested photos of more relatives and Fannie's many friends, some unframed, bent and yellowed with age, others in varied assortment of casings.

Peering into the bedroom, I caught the dim light that streamed through the window across the narrow bed, the shade pulled part-way down. A chenille spread neatly covered a four-postered bed. The back door in the bedroom, the room once utilized as a kitchen, opened into an alley where the dented trash can sat. Staring at the container I thought of all the refuse that has filled its cavity since I have been coming here to separate—to save or discard—my aunt's clothing, papers and household articles.

On the bureau rested treasured photographs representing two generations of my relatives. Decorating the piece of furniture were pictures of my family, my brother Joe's family, and those of my cousins, Rosalie, Millie, and Nora.

A cane stood in the corner of the living room near the front door. Not far from the brown-handled walking stick rested an open folding chair. A beige-colored tam lay on the seat of it, as if a last-minute invitation would find my aunt anxiously departing. Against one wall was a newly acquired blue-striped recliner, still carrying its tags. The electric control on the side lifted its occupant to a standing position, a sad reminder that the petite eighty-seven year old woman who lived in the house for more than half her life could now scarcely cross the room without a walker.

I daydreamed of my aunt in the "old country" as a young girl playing with her sisters, yet undisturbed, laughing with the innocence of a child. And I looked beyond to the seriousness of her maturity, for as she grew older, the deformity that plagued her consciousness loomed larger.

To me, the quiet and humility of her personage was ever beautiful. Auburn hair framed a serene, contented face. Aunt Fannie always assumed a calm, gentle manner, although her piercing brown eyes grew with intensity the few times she did become perturbed. The expression betrayed a customarily subdued nature. A quizzical look furrowed her tweezed brows when the point of a conversation was not clear while at the same time, she prefaced a statement in counterpoint with the question, "You mean to say...?"

Curious and eager to learn, Fannie was a self-educated woman. She did not have the opportunity to attend night school, to study the English language in a classroom, as did many of the new settlers from Eastern Europe. But the brown wooden bookcase standing against her living room wall was assurance that my aunt read best sellers of the day as well as self-help books—books about getting the most out of life.

Sitting on the shelves behind the glass doors were anthologies of short stories, grammar handbooks, writing guides and a frayed dictionary. Many of the books, all kept in good condition, were gifts from friends and relatives, people who knew she was a voracious reader when her eyes were still good. My aunt had purchased a few of the copies, some dog-earred, and many second-hand. Her favorite books which she read and re-read contained collections of stories from Jewish folklore.

Even so, the best story teller, according to my cousins and me, was our own Aunt Fannie. How she captivated her audiences with tales of Czarist Russia, and the struggle for food and survival.

She recounted tales to the young and to the old, and had been telling them for as long as I could remember. And Aunt Fannie recited stories to anyone who would listen. She told stories of history—that of her own and, fundamentally, of her people.

Recapitulating these anecdotes was a way of helping recall the sacrifices the Shulitzky family made, a means of remaining faithful to those memories. It is as if her mission, through detailed repetition of these narratives, was to bequeath her family's suffering to a younger generation— the pain of separation, the years of waiting in anguish—and the fear. It was an experience of survival, and luck, an episode not easily erased from one's very being over the many years.

With each reiteration she validates the durability of my family. The intensity of her voice deludes me. It is as though my ears are hearing the recitations for the first time.

And now I dared to face the question that arose within me: How many more years would my dear aunt be granted? As the question lingered, my mind continued to race. When she dies, an entire generation of blood relatives would be gone—the ancestry of my children, and of my grandchildren.

PART I

ELLIS ISLAND

Chapter One

*A*unt Fannie was the second child of five girls born in Russia to Ethel and Nathan Shulitzky. While Fannie was in her infancy, Ethel noticed that her newborn child no longer kicked her legs about in the same way as she had earlier. Disturbed by this change, concerned that something was radically wrong with the little girl, Ethel imposed upon one of her neighbors to take her and the baby to a hospital in Kiev by horse and wagon. Her worries were not unfounded. After the examination at the hospital, preceded by questions of any recent illnesses, it was determined that Fannie had developed a paralysis on one side of her body which affected her right hip and leg. The diagnosis was poliomyelitis. She would be crippled for life.

Ethel was distraught by this prognosis, but was determined to raise Fannie with the same care and nurturing as she did her first child, and any future children she would bear. During her entire life, Fannie stepped with a limp that controlled her every movement. The muscles in Fannie's right leg were weakened by the disease, and her leg eventually became shorter through a gradual shrinking of the muscles.

The family lived in a small village where everyone

knew everybody. They were poor and there was hardly enough food to keep their stomachs filled. Beets and potatoes were the staples my grandmother cooked to feed her husband and children. When there were a few rubles to buy flour Ethel baked bread.

There came a time when Nathan could no longer support his wife and his family of five daughters with the job of making hefty ropes used on ships. Although, at this time, Jews were still allowed to practice their trades under the Czarist law, Christians were not permitted to supply these materials to craftsmen. Nathan could not obtain the necessary hemp and, hence, could no longer make a living. He sought a better life for his family, away from the destruction of the pogroms which ravaged the lives and property of Russian Jews and drove them out of business. Angry and frustrated, Fannie's father yearned to move to another country so he could earn a decent living for his dependents. Hearing his friends tell of the freedom and financial opportunities in the "golden land" across the ocean, my grandfather ventured to America alone, seeking exile for himself and, eventually, his family. He looked toward opportunities in the new country as dreams fulfilled, and life with absence of fear and oppression.

For a year no one heard from my grandfather.

Many times over, Aunt Fannie told the story of the difficult times they had in the country formerly known as Russia.

"We lived in the Ukraine... it was so backward... had no water, and we used to walk to the river and do the wash. We rarely bathed. If we wanted to wash our clothes, we had to go naked, and we couldn't do that." Trailing off to a whis-

6

per, the embarrassment always bounced from her face.

"There was a Revolution. We had no money, and food was hard to get. So my uncle got my mother a job in a sugar factory cleaning the insides of processing tanks. My mother walked many long miles to work each week. She stayed with the owners of the factory, baking and cooking for them at night, then she would walk home at the end of the week to *Chaschevata, Hyeska.*"

I remember how proudly Aunt Fannie stated the name of the village and the province in which she was born.

Her story would continue, her eyes nostalgic, her voice compelling. "My mother would be carrying thirty pounds of sugar on her back—her week's pay. But we needed flour, not sugar. My mother was able to sell some of the sugar, getting paid in *kerenky* (money named for leader, Alexander F. Kerensky, who served a short term in 1917) and exchange some sugar for salt. My sisters and I were left alone while she worked, and the neighbors would feed us.

It was a hard life."

She described, with despair, how the roof of the house leaked. "When it rained, it rained!" Even so, gratitude shone through her brown eyes while she proclaimed. "But we had a roof over our heads! We persevered, and learned to be considerate of others." Then she added as though in afterthought, aware of the changing values in our country, "I don't think families or schools teach that today," her head shaking from left to right, right to left.

Following a deep sigh, Aunt Fannie told her listeners that, finally, her mother received a letter from Nathan. He settled in Philadelphia, and started a business, a sweater factory.

"After that my father wrote a little more often, but the letters took a long time to reach us," Fannie complained.

In 1913, a few years after he had arrived in America, my grandfather sent money for Gertie, his eldest daughter, to sail to America. She was to make the trip alone. Bubba took her to Kiev to "hook up" with the Hebrew Immigrant Aid Society (HIAS), an organization which helps Jewish immigrants. It was a long, frightening trip for a fourteen year-old traveling to a strange country, leaving her mother and sisters behind. When she arrived in Philadelphia, Gertie boarded with a family in a house apart from her father. She worked in the sweater factory that my grandfather and a partner owned, and like many young immigrants, she had no chance to experience adolescence as many children know it. Fannie, Bella, Rose and Minnie missed their oldest sibling and secretly wondered if they would ever see her again.

"Meanwhile, my youngest sister, Rose, got sick with typhoid fever. She had a high temperature." Pressing ahead with her monologue, the tenor of Aunt Fannie's voice would change. "I was with her. We heard that a doctor was in the area, so I pleaded, 'Rose, don't go to sleep, the doctor is coming soon.' We waited a long, long time but, instead, a neighbor came in. He took a look at Rose. Then he turned to me, gently putting his hands on my shoulders, and in a solemn voice told me my sister had died.

"By 1921 my father was able to send more money for us to go to America. But it was not enough. We had to exchange our house for money so we could travel to America.

"We became *bezhentsy*—refugees—no home, no land."

Chapter Two

*P*ensively, in a low-toned voice, Aunt Fannie echoed stories that now I even know by heart. The stories were told many times over, always with great fervor and in detailed description and, without exception, as though they were unrehearsed.

Aunt Fannie never forgot the starvation she so frequently experienced in her youth in Eastern Europe. She did not want to forget the deprivation and sickness, the scourge of diseases that was rampant. Indebted to life in a country where food was bountiful and soldiers did not line the street, Aunt Fannie felt recompensed having learned self-denial, values, and concerns for other human beings.

"We walked from village to village through Russia, meeting up with one of my aunts and some cousins in another small village quite a distance from where we lived. They knew we didn't have enough money, so they got me a job working for a dressmaker."

Fannie worked day and night sewing buttons and seams, doing what she had learned as a young child. My grandmother had taught her the skill, a way of preparing her for the future—if her lame daughter could earn a living no

9

other way she, at least, could sew. The skill, though tedious with its details, proved valuable. Her fingers were nimble and the hours long.

"'Don't pay her, just feed her,' my mother told the woman. 'It would be one less mouth to feed.'

"A few weeks later, maybe longer, the dressmaker wanted to talk to my mother. I thought maybe I wasn't doing a good job. "'I have a man for whom I make shirts,' whispered the dressmaker to my grandmother. 'I heard he takes people across the border.'

"Later on we were introduced to him as the dressmaker's cousins. She told him that we wanted to get to the border.

"'Fine. If they are your cousins, you pay for them and I'll take them,'" was his answer.

"My mother couldn't afford for all three daughters and herself to go with him. She did not have enough money. So my youngest sister Minnie had to remain behind until some sort of arrangement was worked out for her to join us. She stayed there with our relatives."

It took courage for my grandmother to leave a child behind where, every day, uprisings were taking place and people lay dead in the streets. It took a certain spirit and trust to move across unknown land guided by strangers.

Driven by determination, and looking toward the future, "We crossed more of the country by horse and wagon...started out in the evening to steal ourselves out in the dark. We reached a shack where the man stopped and left us off. Then another man came and led us walking, very fast until we came to a steep hill we had to climb. It was near a river, the Dnestr I think, and we had to get to the shore on the other side."

10

With my aunt's small size and oblique gait, the high mound of land seemed formidable. Fannie felt a swell of panic through her body, a panic which she had never sensed before this very moment. Viewing the almost vertical ground that lay before her, Fannie's screams pierced the silent air. "I can't, I'm going to fall!"

Walking in haste my aunt had fallen countless times in an effort to keep pace with the others. Throughout the journey across the Ukraine land, it was difficult for Fannie to balance herself as she favored the healthy leg to stabilize her body. It taxed her to stay close to the group—the refugees pushing forward—while the threat of being left back in a desolated part of the countryside remained. This time Fannie stood frozen, unable to walk any further. Her mother, following the guide for fear of getting separated from the other escapees, and in an effort not to make any extraneous noises, whispered reassuringly, "Hold onto me, you can make it." Meanwhile, Fannie's feet moved slowly as they trudged upward. She was nearly in shock.

"I was crying," Aunt Fannie admitted each time she retold the experience. Reliving the scene, her words would move at a faster tempo. The refugees advanced up the incline, and trod many more steps until they arrived at the descent.

"It was like a miracle. I found myself picked up in the air, and suddenly I was down the slope!" The challenge was an illusion. Amazed, unable to believe her own powers, Aunt Fannie never failed to exclaim her mystifying bewilderment: "To this day I wonder how I did it!" And a smile of triumph would cross her face.

Terror besieged those refugees who were not sure if they

were going to ever reach America—to see members of their families who had settled there. Apprehension and hunger numbed the excitement of the venture to a new land, but faith, hope and expectations kept them alive. The walking continued, up and down the hills, in the rain and chill of the nights. The days merged into weeks, and the weeks seemed endless. All the while the vigor of Fannie's walking was diminished by the shadow of a limp. That shadow followed the distances she traversed.

There was little food or drink.

"Get in line," they were told.

Panic struck my grandmother when she looked around, gazing into each face, but could not see her youngest daughter anywhere.

"'Ask him where is Bella.'

'You'll find your sister when you go in the building," the stranger promised them.

"Finally we went into a shack with forty, maybe fifty, people sitting around, waiting to get across the river. We looked up and, to our surprise there, in the corner, was Bella. We never knew how she got separated from us.

"A few days passed when a soldier appeared and said, 'We want three people out right now.'

"'Why do you want to kill us one by one?' my mother wailed. My sister, my mother and I came out. To our surprise we were transferred to another shack, and at night we started to walk again. We came to the water where a boat waited every night to take ten or fifteen people across the river. It took us to Romania." The passport received at the Romanian border was the admission ticket to an unfamiliar land—and to freedom. Fannie, Bubba and Bella had left Russia forever, never to return.

In Romania they patiently waited until Minnie joined them, the meeting having been prearranged. Minnie's journey, too, was paid for with money donated from HIAS. My grandmother and the three sisters resumed their travels by train. The cars were crowded, and the stench strong. They did not think about washing their bodies or changing clothes, only of their stomachs which had not gotten used to enduring emptiness.

For the present they felt safe, allowing their voices to rise above a whisper. More days and nights passed. Their journey to a destined seaport was nearly over, crossings of many countries that Aunt Fannie says lasted almost a year. They arrived at the final station, their passports were stamped LONDON, and a mother and her three daughters boarded a ship headed for America.

Thousands of immigrants arrived at Ellis Island every day with their few possessions. The strangers spoke diverse languages and assorted dialects. As each person entered the building, a doctor on duty scanned each foreigner who walked up the stairway. The frightened newcomers were then told to move into pens where they stood in line for hours while waiting to be examined and evaluated. There was an overflow of arrivals whom the officials could not take care of in the course of one day, and many of the immigrants were forced to stay over many nights at a time. Cots were supplied for them to sleep on , and they were well fed.

For days the immigrants passed through the East Wing

of the building where doctors examined every passenger for signs of trachoma, an infectious eye disease. Any foreigner who had the slightest symptom of a contagious or communicable disease, or a detectable diseased heart or lungs, was placed on a ship headed back to his homeland. (The United States Immigration Department forbid entry into the country to persons incapable of caring for themselves, or to anyone who might possibly become a public charge.) There were no distinctions, and a large percentage of the the refugees were sent back to the countries from which they came.

The days of waiting seemed endless. My grandmother's turn finally arrived when she and her three daughters were to be interrogated and physically examined. But one of the daughters limped. There was no way to hide Fannie's deformity, nor to shield her through falsehoods.

Even though the moment of freedom for the four Shulitzky women was close at last, Fannie felt little sense of true freedom within her disfigured body. Ever since she had learned to walk she had been branded by this disability. Her physical handicap lingered undisguised in her consciousness, overtly distinguishable. Fannie's father was always ashamed of her deformity. While she was growing up in Russia her father, in particular, ridiculed her by calling her unpleasant names. She was a disgrace to him.

With the help of a translator, an investigation followed the physical examination. Bubba understood some of the questions, but many she did not. She answered each one the best she could. When the officer reached the bottom of his list and completed the form, he approached Fannie with a piece of white chalk in his hand. Stepping closer, he marked an "X" on her wraps—a move that stigmatized Aunt Fannie for life. She immediately knew she was to be detained and soon deported.

Fannie's young body trembled with agitation. Alarming thoughts raced through her head. If she were sent back to Russia, with whom would she live? Would her mother, or one of her sisters, have to return with her after risking their lives to reach this golden land?

Throughout her life, Fannie's voice shook as she drew a fist to her breast each time she reached this part of her history.

"In my mind I was wondering, 'How could this happen? Is my family to be separated again, this time because of *me*?'"

Yet another miracle occurred for Fannie, an act enough to grant her father forgiveness for his past unkind remarks. Nathan, contacted through HIAS, had been told that his wife and children arrived in New York, but that there was a problem whereas they were not allowed to leave the island. Nathan hurriedly reached Ellis Island to rescue his wife and daughters, taking his older daughter, Gertie, with him.

Although Fannie's father never displayed compassion or fondness for his lame offspring during the years he watched her grow, Nathan thought it a patriarchal obligation to ascertain his second child be allowed to live in this country with her mother and sisters. He assured the officer in authority that he would take care of Fannie, and that she was capable of working for him in his sweater factory. He assured him with the money he casually slipped into the official's hand.

Gertie, in the meantime, was made to wait on the first floor in the cavernous building that brought back memories

15

of her own entrance into America in the years before. She thought she saw her sisters on the balcony above, and waved furiously to catch their attention. Bella and Minnie, looking down from the second story, were at odds whether that particular woman below, trying desperately to get their attention, was truly their oldest sister. It had been eight years since they had seen each other. They hardly recognized the gangling girl who had since developed into womanhood. At last, a mother and four sisters were together once more, the hugs interspersed with fountains of tears.

It was 1921 when the Shulitzky family was reunited—except for Rose who lay in a grave in Russia.

Chapter Three

A new life for the family was beginning. They had settled in a young country where millions of immigrants from
many Eastern European countries had come in search of
human rights and peace—and their fortune. How proud the
family was when, that day in March of 1922, Nathan, Ethel,
Minnie, Bella and Fannie became American citizens. Aunt
Fannie thought that once they reached America the difficult
times for her family would be over.

Nathan and Ethel set up housekeeping with their four
daughters in a rowhouse on Poplar Street, a quiet neighborhood near a main thoroughfare in Philadelphia. The big decisions were made by the male head of the household. His
wife and daughters lived in fear of the short, surly cigar-
smoking tyrant. Bubba, a sweet, gentle woman, whose hair
was already showing strains of gray, quietly carried out the
tasks of a typical housewife. She stayed at home to cook and
care for her family once more, but found time to gossip with
the neighbors. Life was easier for Bubba in the new land.

The area in which the family had settled was populated
mostly with Jewish people from Eastern Europe. A synagogue, serving as a social, as well as a religious, meeting

17

place was founded nearby where members of the congregation worshiped without fear. That former apprehension was one of many hardships lifted from the shoulders of the immigrants in their adopted land.

Modestly furnished, the house contained enough comforts to keep the women content. The family felt rich with its meager possessions—luxuries to them—after surviving in Russia with not even so much as bare necessities. Eventually the family purchased a sewing machine to make new clothes and mend the old. A few years later an upright piano was added to the small living room, although no one ever played it.

In anticipation of the evening's dinner, Bubba now could walk to the fish market where live fish often swam in the cool water. The dairy store which sold fresh eggs, butter, sour cream and cheese, stood next door. Located on the same block was the butcher shop, supplying only kosher meats inspected by the rabbi, and everyone could always smell the bakery down the street. There was nothing tastier, nor more tender, than the rye bread with caraway seeds, warm from the oven.

Marketing was convenient, the food fresh and abundant. Horse-pulling vendors sold their produce from wagons, and on a hot summer day "Ice for sale!" was yelled through the streets by the iceman who sold both dry ice and frozen blocks. The ice was essential to keep food from spoiling in those days in what was known as "iceboxes." The umbrella repairman traveled from neighborhood to neighborhood fixing the damaged rain protectors, and a man who sharpened knives and scissors followed close behind. As long as a family had money enough to take advantage of the choices of foodstuffs and services available to them, life in America was good.

At age seventeen Fannie started to work for her father as had been promised the immigration officer who gave permission for her to pass through the gates at Ellis Island. Fannie learned the process of finishing sweaters. Bella and Minnie, too, worked in the factory stitching sweaters together.

Gertie continued her job in the knitting mill for the many years since her father had opened the shop. She had made numerous friends from the time she had landed in this country, and when she was twenty-two years old, a suitor asked for her hand in marriage. Her prospective husband, Thomas Hamburg, barely made a living working for the railroad. Still, he and Gertie, very much in love, married. It was the interval of time in America when, through marriage to a man who had already secured his citizenship, a newly-wedded woman automatically became a citizen.

Soon after they were married, Thomas changed jobs. His father-in-law had invited him to work as a bookkeeper in the sweater factory. With Thomas earning more money, the young couple was now able to afford a house, and purchased a house around the corner from Ethel and Nathan. Within a year their household was active with a baby whom they named Joseph. It was an exciting period of time for the family as each member doted on the first American-born child. Nathan was in a state of bliss. A boy amidst all those women!

Shortly after Joseph's birth, though, an altercation between Thomas and Nathan ended Thomas's job at the factory. Thomas was forced to seek a different job to feed his small family. With a little savings, Gertie and Thomas

19

decided to move to a small, growing town in South Jersey on the recommendation of some Russian friends who had settled there. It was the same town in which they had spent their short honeymoon. With money borrowed from the bank, they opened a dry-goods store.

The Shulitzky Family with Joseph sitting in front of Gertie.

Minnie, in America for only a short while, soon fell in love, also. Minnie was the most attractive of the four sisters. She and Harry were married in her parents' house when she was seventeen years old. Harry was a hard working businessman with an easy-going disposition. The newlyweds lived with Ethel and Nathan before they moved into the apartment above Harry's butcher shop. Harry had previously bought the building which housed several stores and some second-story apartments. Five years after their marriage their first child was born, a daughter Rosalie, named for Rose.

20

During these years, economic stability in the United States started to waver as the country headed toward the Great Depression of 1929. After many years in business, Nathan, unable to pay his debts, was forced to close the sweater factory. He had lost everything. The loss of his business aggravated his asthma, and from then on his health began to fail. He could no longer work a full day, and jobs were limited, if any were available. Fannie and Bella were also out of work at a time when the family's scant savings were quickly shrinking, and the reality of a dream began to fade. For the first time, money had become scarce for the family that had a taste of the good life in America.

Since two of the daughters had married, Jewish tradition deemed that it become the responsibility of the oldest child who lived at home to financially support the household. Fannie realized she had to get a job. So she applied for work at another sweater factory. Though aware of her capability of working on the end process of completing sweaters, a sprinkle of skepticism trickled through her confidence: she wondered if she could hold a responsible job with strangers *because of my condition.*

Telling about how she got work was always one of Aunt Fannie's favorite stories.

"I can always work with my hands," she would reaffirm with pride, extending her hands palms up, both elbows resting on her hips. This dramatization occurred with each repetition of her unswerving declaration.

Waiting to apply for a job at another sweater factory, for what seemed an interminable amount of time Fannie, at long last, found herself at the front of the extended line. In

21

a reserved voice she would remark how she was the spokesperson not only for herself, but for all the other people seeking work.

"The man who did the hiring walked up to me, and without warning said, 'I'm sorry but all of the jobs are taken.'" Feeling discouraged, not only for herself but for all the other women who were in line behind her, Fannie readily retorted, "You mean to tell me that all of these people have to go away without getting a job?

"'Are you experienced?'" asked the man in charge.

Anxious for the chance to prove her worthiness, and the right to earn a living just as well as anyone else, Fannie spoke up with resounding resolution. "Of course I'm experienced. I'm a sweater finisher."

The man, who just a few seconds ago had almost turned her away, was caught off-guard. He immediately directed Fannie to a foreman who, in turn, gave her some sweaters to complete.

She then described how "I picked up the garment and studied what I'm supposed to do." Immediately her tone changed.

"My father manufactured light sweaters, not heavy ones like these." An attitude of defeat was now evident in her voice. "I never worked on this kind of sweater in my life."

After Fannie candidly told the foreman that this was not the kind of garment she had been used to completing, he asked, "Who did you work for?" testing the truth of her prior convictions.

"I gave the foreman the name of my father's company—Bell Knitting Mills.

"'Bell Knitting Mills? he repeated.'" The pitch of her voice would swing upward in recollection of the foreman's reaction. "'I wouldn't be surprised if the owner himself didn't know what to do with it.'

"He then directed me to 'Go over there and tell the forelady to teach you and not to let you go until you know it well.' That was how I was trained."

Aunt Fannie worked at the factory for over two years doing what is still called *piece* work. "The faster we worked, the more money we made. But the quality of my work mattered more than how many sweaters I could finish in a day. The forelady would say, 'She turns out a garment that is a pleasure to look at.' The other workers skipped a stitch here and a stitch there. I made only eight dollars a week."

Fannie must have done a good job for, with a chuckle, she liked to tell about the raise she unknowingly received." One time there was twelve dollars in my pay, so I asked my father, 'Shall I go to the office and tell them they made a mistake?'" It was difficult for Fannie to believe that a stranger was truly satisfied with the garments she turned out, so much so that he wanted to give her a salary increase.

"She just came to this country and already she knows more than the bookkeeper," her father said, poking fun at his scrupulous daughter. But her father took the money to use for household expenses, leaving Fannie with very little of her earnings.

Not too long after Fannie got the raise, Nathan was seized with a fatal heart attack. Now that the man of the house was gone, the responsibility of supporting my grandmother was solely up to Fannie. Although Bella offered a portion of her earnings from work, Minnie and Harry deemed it an obligation to contribute to the welfare of Minnie's mother and unmarried sisters. As much as Gertie and Thomas wanted to do their part, they were unable to help financially. Somehow the family managed, as did many families during the Depression.

When Bella finished work she attended night school. Both she and Minnie attended the free classes designed specifically for families of Jewish immigrants. Since Yiddish was the predominant language spoken in the house, they felt it important to take advantage of the opportunity to learn to read and write English. Now living in America, they wanted to speak the language of their adopted country.

Bella took the time and patience to teach her sister Fannie the alphabet in English, and phonetics just as she was learning them. Fannie attempted to translate Russian words into English and tried to pronounce them correctly. With the added help of a kind neighbor, she read words from the newspaper. Thomas, who had previously attended night school, taught his persistent sister-in-law how to write and, subsequently, spell words in a language that, at one time, was strange to her. Fannie, with her thirst for learning, was overjoyed to receive the fragment of education once denied her and all the other poor, young Jewish girls in the "old country."

At the urging of Gertie, who never learned to read or write, Thomas continued to work with his sister-in-law until she had advanced her skills enough to read at an elementary level. Gertie, too, realized that of all the siblings, Fannie was going to have to make her own way in the world, and it was mandatory that my aunt learn to read and write English. Ironically, for herself, Gertie relied upon her husband to read articles from the newspapers and other magazines to her. Gertie did, however, learn elementary mathematics, sufficient enough to manage the dry goods business she and Thomas operated for their entire lives.

Gertie and Thomas were happy in their business. It provided them with a good living and perhaps served as an inspiration for Aunt Fannie, as well. With the encouragement of her older sister and brother-in-law, Aunt Fannie left the job of finishing sweaters and searched for a location to open a business of her own.

That was in 1928, the same year I, Edward, was born to Thomas and Gertie Hamburg.

PART II

COLUMBIA AVENUE

Chapter Four

*F*annie was twenty-five years old. She had been in America for eight years. Thinking of the huge undertaking, and the overwhelming responsibility of running a business, many doubts ran through her mind. Fannie contemplated how a person with a handicap, no less a woman, could manage a store standing on her feet for long periods of time. Fannie knew she couldn't afford to hire help at the outset. She also wondered about her own competence in ordering merchandise and keeping financial accounts. Yet Fannie relished the idea of being self-employed and establishing her independence after working many years for someone else. The more she deliberated, the more the family convinced her to attempt the undertaking. She knew that her sisters and brothers-in-law were ready to stand by and be her advisors. Fannie, in making a final decision, rationalized that "If my family has faith in me, then I know I can do it." Yet, her instinct speculated on how customers would look upon her physical appearance and react to the slow shuffling of her feet.

After much mental confusion, and coercion, Fannie announced to the family that she was going to risk the endeavor of running a business alone. She decided it was in her own best interest to overlook the fact that customers would be aware of her limp—to try not to think of herself—although the self-consciousness lingered in her mind as much as in her legs. It was important that she earn a living for herself and her mother. With good wishes from her sisters and brothers-in-law, Fannie set out to demonstrate her family's faith in her. And she was determined to prove herself worthy of being an American, an obligation she was proud of. She had no intentions of letting anyone down.

Harry owned the building on Columbia Avenue which housed his butcher shop and an adjacent store. Conveniently, it was empty, and proved to be an ideal location. Above the businesses was an apartment in which Minnie and Harry lived, and Fannie liked the idea of having family nearby. She paid rent to Harry for the space. With recommendations from my parents, Aunt Fannie ordered fixtures and merchandise to start on her new venture. In 1928 Fannie opened the *National Five Cent & Ten Cent Store*.

The dimensions of the store next to the butcher shop were narrow, and not very deep. It was, however, ideal for a sole individual who was not used to walking back and forth from one end of the store to the other, waiting on customers and filling in stock. Counters and shelves lined two walls of the store. Sets of dishes, and pots and pans were displayed on one side, boxes reaching high to the ceiling. Rolls of printed fabric, and various colors of oilcloth by the yard, lined the wall on the opposite side of the floor, as well as boxes containing window shades. Aunt Fannie stocked other items which replicated the dry goods that Gertie and Tom carried in their small business such as sheets, towels, and curtains.

A black-iron treadle sewing machine sat in the back of the store. Operated by foot, the machine was a convenience when, during a lull midst business hours, Fannie took the opportunity to mend her clothes, and often those of her mother. Also, with fabric from the store, she turned out new garments for herself. The sewing cabinet, when closed, doubled as a table where my aunt ate her meals which had been prepared by my grandmother. A single electric burner to heat soup, or water for tea sat on a small table nearby. Mealtime for Aunt Fannie, though, came at no specific hour. She ate whenever she remembered, for she rarely felt hunger while occupied with customers or displaying merchandise, or concentrating on sewing.

In the rear of the store was a short door behind which was a cubbyhole. Here papers, bills, checkbooks and other records were stored in metal boxes. My aunt somehow managed to creep inside the small space with her off-balance body, and with the use of a flashlight she was able to retrieve something she needed. She would never resort to asking anyone, not even a family member who might be in the store at the time, to get what she wanted. This was the beginning of her virtual independence, as I recall. Fannie never wanted to impose on someone else what she could do for herself.

Several times a year my aunt attempted to place "specials" in the display window hoping to catch a customer's eye, bringing him or her into the store to make a purchase. The space in the window was another area in which Fannie found it difficult to maneuver. Strategically placing merchandise often meant bending at awkward angles for minutes at a

time, and then Fannie would have to crawl out to get something she may have forgotten, or stop to wait on a customer.
Standing up straight in the seven by one-and-one-half foot
space was almost impossible for her, no less to be careful not
to lose her balance and fall against the glass window.

There was no bathroom in the store. Fannie had access
to the toilet in her sister's living quarters which had an
entrance from the outside. This meant that whenever Fannie
wanted to make use of the bathroom, it was necessary for
her to walk outside to lock up the store, and walk next door.
As she made her way up the high-angled steps in the darkened stairwell, her uneven motion cast a curious silhouette
on the diagonal wall.

On most Sundays my parents drove to the wholesalers'
in downtown Philadelphia to buy merchandise before visit-
ing Bubba and Aunt Fannie. Frequently they drove first to
West Philadelphia to pick up Fannie and take her with them.
If my aunt had an unusually large order, my father would
then drive to Fannie's store in North Philadelphia to drop
off the purchase. By that time of the day, my aunts and
uncles had already congregated at Bubba's house, where my
grandmother was preparing her special Sunday dinner.

While they were at Fannie's place of business, Gertie
and Thomas often studied how Fannie laid out her merchandise and gave their suggestions. They also offered con-
structive criticism on the window display, for which Fannie
was grateful. Although my aunt saved shipping costs when
Thomas delivered the merchandise, no one thought about
the wear and tear on his Pontiac, or my gray-haired father
who tirelessly drove back to New Jersey at the end of the

day. He always seemed cooperative, ready and willing to help my aunt even after working in his own business six days a week. Treating Aunt Fannie as he would his own sister, he never seemed to complain. This was now the only family my father had.

Thomas was born in the Ukraine, also. He arrived in America with his only sister Anna just years before Gertie came to this country. Anna had married and died at an early age leaving three children who were placed in an orphanage. I know my father was happy to be a part of the Shulitzky family, and enjoyed his brothers-in-law's banter. He was especially good to Fannie, as well, for my mother's sake.

Once in a while my parents ordered extra rolls of fancy gift-wrapping paper from a paper distributor, and shared it with my aunt. When they delivered it to her, accompanying the paper were bows my mother made from lengths of ribbon to decorate the wrapped packages. The fancy ribbons were an incentive for Fannie's customers to buy their gifts from her—a good selling device, she admitted.

Aunt Fannie enjoyed reminiscing about her first trip to the wholesaler to buy merchandise on credit. It was a story she remembered well and delighted in repeating, adding her deepest appreciation to my parents who were with her.

Thomas and Gertie informed Mr. Ormann, the owner of a wholesale business downtown, that Fannie wanted to buy some merchandise to open a store, but was unable to pay him until she reaped a profit. Mr. Ormann indignantly insisted, "I can't give her credit. I don't even know if she'll be able to pay her bills or not."

Thomas at once vouched for her credit saying, "You

send the bills on my name. I'll see that you get your money." Fannie could not believe she heard those words from Thomas. She reveled in the confidence her brother-in-law assumed in her.

As the weeks passed, Fannie insisted on knowing "When will the bills come in on my name?"

"Don't worry about it," Thomas answered. "Just sell the merchandise." Such venerable trust her sister and brother-in-law held in her further obligated my aunt to do well in her business. Then and there my aunt's belief in herself was secured.

The telephone wires were busy between the small town in New Jersey and the Columbia Avenue address while my parents and Aunt Fannie exchanged ideas. Choices were discussed, and decisions were made. The deliberations were an excuse, also, for Fannie and my mother to telephone each other.

Aunt Fannie's dark eyes always lit up when she told how, months later she opened her mail at the store. Quickly Fannie dialed her eldest sister's out-of-town telephone number. My mother, lifting the receiver to her ear, was interrupted before she even finished saying "Hello." In an instant she heard the excitement in Fannie's voice.

"I got a bill, I got a bill," blurted Fannie. Pausing, she thought to finish her sentence, ..."on my name."

Her credit was established. My aunt had become experienced in determining the type of merchandise that won patrons for her, and in helping customers with their selections. Now a respected business woman. Fannie's customers became her friends, often stopping by if only to say "hello." Salesmen came into the store to inquire if Fannie needed any of their specialities. They wanted to sell her new items on the market, or suggest merchandise they thought would sell well in that particular neighborhood.

Circular of the First Anniversary Sale held in 1929

Celebrating her initial year in business, my aunt held a First Anniversary Sale. She had circulars printed, and distributed them to her customers who, in turn, advertised the news to their friends and relatives. The circulars brought Fannie new customers. After the first year in business she no longer worried about paying the bills. With an ensured income, and having learned to write checks, the invoices were paid on time. Her credit with wholesalers reached a high rating. She was, in fact, able to periodically put money into a savings account.

The responsibility of keeping the store open six days a week, caring for customers, displaying her wares, and changing window displays, filled Fannie's days. The bones in my aunt's body felt the toll of tasks at the end of each day, but it was rewarding to know that she was working for herself, and all the effort she exerted in making a living gave her that boundless satisfaction.

In the heat of summer, the cold of the winter, in torrents of rain and falling snow, my aunt traveled to work. The woman who scuffled along with a limp alighted two separate trolleys for many years. Each morning she greeted the same passengers going to work, and on those rare days when she didn't appear her fellow passengers sensed something was amiss for, following an absence, they always asked her how she was and why she missed going to work.

Since I had had experience waiting on customers, and filling in stock in my parent's business when I was in high school, Gertie and Thomas suggested I help Aunt Fannie during holidays and summer vacations. I traveled on the bus from our town in New Jersey to Philadelphia, and then transferred to the number of the trolley that ran right past Aunt Fannie's store.

I looked forward to spending the day with my aunt because she always wanted to treat me. My greatest joy was to buy a hot dog and soda, with money she gave me, from the Texas Weiner Shop next door. I can still smell the odor of the small sausages encased in soft rolls wafting through the summertime air. Spending time with my aunt was one of the pleasant memories of my boyhood.

My cousin Rosalie, too, whose family had since moved to the suburbs when she was ready to start school, worked in Aunt Fannie's store. Our aunt was overflowing with uncommon happiness when her niece and nephew spent a day with her. She always found a job for us to do, usually giving Rosalie the task of folding and piling the stock neatly in bins on the counters. But Rosalie did not always complete her job, for her fun was running back and forth from Aunt Fannie's *Five and Ten* to her father's butcher shop and back again. Rosalie spent the hours between the two stores until her father closed the butcher shop in the evening. Then both she and Aunt Fannie rode home with Uncle Harry.

My brother Joe, now reaching over six feet, worked next door to Aunt Fannie's store in our uncle's butcher shop on weekends. He never seemed to take much interest in the dry goods business. As he was attending Temple University at the time, he roomed at Bubba's house which made traveling to school convenient for him, as well as convenient to get to work. He worked for Uncle Harry until he enlisted in the service in 1942, a year after World War II broke out.

Bella, the youngest of the four sisters, helped Fannie on Saturdays until she met Paul, her future husband. She met him nine years after Fannie had opened her store. Bella was a petite, docile woman, approaching her forties. During their courtship Paul worked in a fish store. Soon after their wedding he decided to open a variety store in South Philadelphia, and Bella worked along with him building up their new business. She and Paul then left Bubba's house, where they lived after their marriage, and moved to a developing section of homes in the suburbs. Their new address was a few blocks from Minnie's and Harry's house.

Paul, an aggressive businessman, eventually opened a wholesale warehouse. For a while he kept his first business flourishing. The successful entrepreneur conveniently became one of Aunt Fannie's suppliers, making personal deliveries to the Columbia Avenue store. Paul also delivered merchandise, which my parents had ordered from him, to my grandmother's house on Sundays for their convenience. As his wholesale business grew more successful, he sold the retail store, and concentrated on his latter endeavor.

An exchange of merchandise constantly took place between the in-laws—the three business owners. The trading proved to be advantageous for, if an item did not sell well at one store, there was a better chance it would sell at an in-law's store location.

Fannie was indebted, having gained three brothers-in-law on whom she could rely for advice and encouragement, and deliveries and transportation. Thomas, Harry, and Paul each unbegrudgingly assisted my aunt in different ways. Despite their help, Fannie remained independent regarding the responsibilities her business demanded.

Ours was a typical close-knit immigrant family. How

well I remember each Sunday. Without fail, a ritual gathering of aunts and uncles, along with their growing families, took place. The majority of the meetings were at my grandmother's house where siblings and spouses and their children came to talk, and eat. No matter if one of the couples was invited elsewhere, a party or a wedding, they stopped first at Bubba's house.

With great pleasure, Bubba spent most of Sunday in the kitchen cooking and baking. There was always enough food for anyone who dropped in—and visitors they did have. Friends and relatives of even the in-laws were welcome to share the ample supply of the good hot-cooked meals. Not everyone ate at the same time; people seemed to drop in, then leave. Dining often took up the whole afternoon while my grandmother stood in the kitchen, unmindful of what was taking place in the living room, avoiding the conversations and, most often, arguments that kindled amongst the sisters.

Bella and Minnie walked into the kitchen to fill platters for their husbands and children, cafeteria style. Someone always carried Fannie's dinner to the dining room table after she was seated. Then later, one or two of my aunts helped my grandmother wash and dry dishes. Somehow, Fannie was never one of them.

Occasionally, Minnie invited the family to her house. She cooked a tasty meal, and we enjoyed the time spent there. We seldom went to Bella's home. I don't know why. My parents took turns as hosts a few times during the year. My mother was not the best of cooks, and since she was tired after working in the store six days a week, she was not expected to prepare meals for the whole family. So on their

37

way to New Jersey, with Bubba and Aunt Fannie in the car, whichever uncle was driving stopped to buy some delicatessen, fresh rye bread and pastries. That was always a real treat.

After arriving at my parents' apartment, located above the business, Aunt Fannie purposely walked down the steps leading into the store, often followed by Thomas. She browsed around to get ideas of how Thomas and Gertie displayed their merchandise, and to check prices of items similar to those she sold.

Sunday's discussions usually covered business, politics, and ultimately the war, though the mainstay of the conversations was gossip. "Penny-ante" was the highlight of each Sunday evening. The game drew my aunts and uncles around the table like magnets, no matter in whose house the family gathered. Cigarette smoke clouded the dining room air while the game progressed through spurts of laughter.

I noticed that, without fail, Fannie had no desire to join her sisters and brothers-in-law who were gambling for the small stakes. Preferring to sit on the sofa in the living room she, instead, engrossed herself in a book which rested on her lap, her head bent forward, her feet barely touching the floor.

As Rosalie and I grew older we, too, sat on the sofa, and interrupted Aunt Fannie's reading. It was then that our aunt started to tell us the stories of life in Russia, and her family's escape to America. We were mesmerized with her storytelling. Yet, as a young boy, it was difficult for me to realize these truths occurred only within the last generation.

When Rosalie stayed overnight at Bubba's house, she took pleasure climbing into bed with Aunt Fannie and listening to the tales that seemed so vivid with details that only Aunt Fannie could supply—and facts often unsuited for a young child. But any fears that stirred within my cousin were allayed with hugs and kisses from a loving aunt.

By this time, Rosalie had become a big sister. Another girl, named Mildred, was born to Minnie and Harry almost immediately after they had moved into their new house.

It is said that bad news sometimes accompanies joyful announcements, or vice versa. Soon after Millie, as the family called her, was born, the family learned that their older daughter displayed symptoms of a debilitating disease: juvenile diabetes.

The doctors assured Minnie that, with proper diet and a regulated program of insulin, Rosalie would live a normal childhood and mature into adulthood. The young child with the dark ringlets, one month older than I, would have to be monitored carefully, and eventually learn to self-administer the syringe filled with insulin. Minnie and Harry hoped to raise Rosalie with the same discipline they would administer to any other child who was disease free. They were certain to oversee her diet and attend to her medication. A huge responsibility, which caused a great deal of anxiety among my emotional family members, had befallen my aunt and uncle. The sisters, however, seemed to thrive on illnesses and dreadful happenings.

My cousins and I got into trouble when we played at Bubba's house. Rosalie and I liked to play games—checkers and Parcheesi—at the top of the stairs. Millie would climb up the steps and, with her arm, clear the pieces from their strategically thought-out places. This made us angry, but we got back at her with teasing, taunting, and arguing.

We were not the only ones who argued, however. Misinterpretations, misunderstandings and jealousy caused much conflict between Fannie, Bella, and Minnie. Guilty of offering unsolicited advice, Aunt Fannie often became the victim of disparaging remarks which, in turn, provoked her enough to speak up in defense. Other times she would remain silent and uninvolved, allowing her two sisters who lived nearby to continue the tirades between themselves.

My grandmother, unable to tolerate the discord, pretended to ignore what was taking place around her. She avoided intervening with the knowledge that she could not be helpful in maintaining peace. Bubba relied on my mother, the eldest of the four sisters, and most often the impartial observer, to be the mediator on her Sunday visits. Sunday was the day of arbitration.

Gertie was a tall woman who towered over her small-framed sisters. Though she appeared overbearing with her ample body, her personality represented an antithesis to her appearance. Gertie sustained competence to control such situations with great insight. Although Minnie and Bella resented her interference, they listened to, and respected their older sister. Seldom did they raise their voice to her.

The quarreling, however, did not interfere with the men, who had no need for emotional engagements. They left the women to their grievances while they continued their friendly discussions, and acknowledged each others' opinions. Harry, Thomas, and Paul found enough to talk about to keep their conversations spirited: Pearl Harbor, gas rationing, and food stamps. They spoke of the employment rate and their prospering businesses during the war years. My brother Joe, and his tour of service, became a passionate topic during their discussions. And when the dialogue waned, one of my uncles most certainly would drift off into a catnap.

Chapter Five

*I*t was the year 1943 that my brother Joe was on the other side of the world risking his life for the sake of freedom—the very freedom for which our grandparents had risked their lives. My brother had been sent to China, and news from China arrived infrequently. When my parents received a letter from Joe, it was brief. Since mail was censored during the war, we had no idea exactly where he was located. Concern for him reached an anxious level amongst all of us, and though the spats between my aunts continued as usual, the uneasiness about their nephew brought the whole clan closer together.

The interval was an especially difficult time for Gertie and Thomas. A year or so before Joe enlisted in the service, the doctors discovered that my mother was suffering from heart disease. She was dependent on her medication, and devoted to the doctor who kept her alive. For the remainder of her life, she was forced to limit her activities, and the added stress of worriment about her first born was detrimental to her health.

Despite the gloom that settled over the lives of my parents, a streak of sunshine appeared through the years of gray clouds which illness, separation of war, and family tensions had brought. Bella gave birth to a daughter. Bubba and Aunt Fannie lived some of their happiest moments watching Nora develop through the stages of childhood. The radiance of a new baby in the family offset a tendency toward despondence.

The hovering clouds dispersed when Joe returned home from three years of service in China. My parents found out, after the war was over and Joe had been home for a while, that a Catholic priest from Philadelphia, who served as a missionary in China, had hidden their eldest son and some of his buddies in a parish. The priest offered them a haven when their lives were endangered by Japanese infiltrations onto the Chinese mainland.

There was plenty to be thankful for when this hero landed in the United States, safe from the secret mission to which he had been assigned, in good health but thinner. My parents could barely contain their excitement, yearning to see their son after years of worry and prayer. They could not wait to celebrate their son's homecoming. My parents planned a grand party for the occasion, anxious to share their happiness with friends and family. The party was to be held the first weekend after his arrival home.

My grandmother already had prepared her delicious home-made grape wine in anticipation of her grandson's homecoming. However, as the turn of events would have it, she was not at Joe's homecoming celebration. Nor were her other daughters and their husbands. The date of the party was scheduled for the same day as Millie's marriage.

This was a very special occasion for Gertie and Thomas.

They wanted to rejoice. Joe's safe arrival home took precedence over any other family celebration for it had been three years since they last saw their eldest son whose life was at stake while on special assignment. My parents' thoughts were filled only with joy and happiness for their son and for themselves. They did not propose to postpone the party, and proceeded to schedule the event the evening of the wedding.

Since Bella had already made her commitment to Minnie, and Aunt Fannie and Bubba depended on Bella and Paul to drive them to the hall where Millie's wedding was to take place, Aunt Fannie and Bubba were obligated to attend the ceremony. Hearts were torn. Gertie and Minnie were separated by silence that lasted for weeks. Consideration for Gertie's health, and the elation of having their nephew home alive gradually soothed the situation between the two sisters, no doubt at the coaxing of my grandmother. While this was the only major clash that occurred between Gertie and any one of her sisters, the relationship between Minnie and my mother was never the same as it had been.

It wasn't until a few months later that the routines of the three families slid into a continuum day in and day out. And the weekly visits to Bubba's continued on schedule until Bubba died.

Jewish neighbors, who were very much a part of the neighborhood where Bubba and Aunt Fannie lived, started to move to outlying sections of Philadelphia. As a result of my other aunts' changes of location, it was expected that

Fannie and my grandmother sell their house on Poplar Street, pack their possessions, and move closer to Minnie and Bella and their families. In March, 1947, Bubba and Aunt Fannie resettled in West Philadelphia, in a section of rowhouses where the porches overlooked one another.

The house on Malvern Avenue was near the corner, convenient to the bus stop. Aunt Fannie had fewer steps to walk, but it was once again necessary for her to change vehicles to reach her destination.

Bella and Paul, and Minnie and Harry contributed generously to the domestic comforts of Fannie and Bubba in their new home. They provided them with additional furniture, and bought conveniences for the kitchen to facilitate Bubba's cooking.

Although the families were closer in proximity, the intangible distance between the sisters widened through the years as sporadic arguments ignited. Hurt feelings turned into grudges, lasting for weeks at a time, whenever one of my aunts felt manipulated. Bubba, who was growing older and less patient with her daughters' intimidating remarks directed at each other, resolved to ignore the resultant disputes. The lack of communication between the angry sisters greatly distressed my grandmother and uninvolved sisters. There was not much Bubba could say or do, and my mother could no longer jeopardize her health by interfering, which left the women to fend for themselves. Two of the sisters coordinated their visits to Bubba's house so that whoever was not on speaking terms, as it were, arrived at alternate times. It made for an awkward situation if one of them was not talking to Aunt Fannie, or vice versa.

46

But the three brothers-in-law continued their conversations as usual. The topics turned towards their businesses, such as mark-ups and gains and losses, and the better-selling merchandise. Thomas, Harry, and Paul were always available for consultation whenever Fannie had a question or problem concerning her store. They advised her on many things—taxes, investments and finances in general. They advised her on buying new items for the store and how to get rid of the old; how to keep a low inventory and continue to make a profit. Fannie recognized that her brothers-in-law understood her better than her two younger sisters ever did. Her brothers-in-law criticized her unjudgmentally, and without condescension, and she accepted their criticism in good favor.

Meanwhile, Fannie sat as an observer of her sisters' marriages. She recounted that Gertie, Bella, and Minnie each had a family, and each sister had her own social circle. Harry and Paul were members of a men's fraternal lodge. The couples' lives seemed complete. Her two younger sisters, especially, had everything in the way of materialistic possessions and luxuries they ever needed or wanted—things they could never have imagined owning in their youth in Russia. I know my mother was satisfied with the limited wealth she and my father worked so hard to accumulate during their marriage. Often, and with puzzlement, Fannie viewed, through the lens of her mind's telescope, the complaints she heard from Minnie and Bella involving differences of opinions between themselves and their husbands. Actually there were no major problems between the couples to speak of, but my aunt ascertained that all spouses should get along amicably, no matter what minor problems they surmounted. There was no doubt Fannie was envious of her sisters, each of whom had a spouse to share a lifetime with. She could not understand why Minnie and Bella frequently appeared dissatisfied with their lives. Moreover, they had no physical affliction with which to contend. It was ironic, just the same, that Minnie and Bella were jealous of their single sister. They envied Fannie because she had no responsibilities other than to herself and her mother.

Advancing into her fortieth year, Fannie had long matured to spinsterhood. Marriage seemed to have bypassed her all of those years. Was there any hope for Fannie?

Referring to her lameness, she questioned, "Who would marry me in my 'condition?'" Grasping on to hope then, Fannie wondered, should a man ask for her hand in marriage, would he do so out of compassion?

Fannie tried to stay involved with her business and the family, keeping many thoughts to herself. She had also cultivated friends of her own, having become acquainted with Sonia when they both lived in the same neighborhood on Poplar Street. After Sonia married and moved to Rhode Island, Fannie and Sonia kept in contact with each other. Sonia visited Philadelphia occasionally, bringing her young son Ben with her. My aunt was extremely affected when people came to see her—the fact that they took time out of their day to spend exclusively with her touched her deeply. I know she always became excited to see an old friend, for over the years a special kinship developed between a few of her dear admirers. With the passing of time, Sonia and she became as close as sisters, as Aunt Fannie watched Ben grow into manhood. To him she was always known as "Aunt Fannie."

Gradually, a friendship evolved, also, between Fannie and Eugene, a wholesaler, whom my parents had introduced to Fannie. Fannie began to buy merchandise from this new supplier. Either my parents drove with Fannie to his place of business on Sundays or Eugene stopped into Fannie's store mid-week to see if she needed to order any items for the store. Eugene's visits became more and more frequent. (I wonder if this was his excuse to see my aunt.)

Her suitor, like Aunt Fannie, was short and approximately my aunt's age—in his forties. His deformed back was plainly visible. He impressed Aunt Fannie as being kind and considerate through the long conversations they held at her store. One of those conversations led to a proposal of marriage. Eugene wanted Fannie to be his wife! Fannie was flattered. Had someone envisioned spending the rest of his life with her? Unprepared for such an offer, she wanted time to give the invitation serious consideration. She knew from their talks that he had children, and she wondered how she could adjust to an established family.

Was it a matter of love, or convenience? What about the store and financial arrangements? How would her mother fit into the picture? There were too many matters to be considered, questions that she hadn't even thought of at that moment. Did she really love him enough to be his wife, or would love blossom through their compatibility? Was it necessary for someone to be in love for a marriage to be successful?

Fannie picked up the telephone receiver several times,

then put it down again. Fannie was so excited she immediately wanted to tell her mother about the proposal, but she decided to wait until she got home from work. She wanted to discuss the situation in length after sorting out her feelings for this man.

When my aunt arrived home that evening, she broke through her greeting with the startling news. It was a few days later, during numerous discussions with her mother, that Bubba forthrightly spoke her opinion. She did not want Fannie to marry Eugene, and sought to discourage her single daughter.

"It sounds like he only wants a mother for his children." Fannie's head was whirling. She tried to weigh every issue carefully. She knew Eugene was a worthy, honest man who made a comfortable living and would be able to take care of her, but the more Fannie thought and talked about it, the more confused she became. She did not want to hurt her mother by marrying him against her better judgement and started to believe that perhaps Bubba was right after all. Nor did Fannie want to disappoint Eugene. She tried to delay her answer to Eugene until she was absolutely certain of a decision. She knew how much he longed for companionship since losing his first wife. In the meantime, her suitor was pressing for a response, one that would determine each of their future.

After much pondering, Fannie reached a verdict. She was going to turn down Eugene's offer. She decided it was better for both herself and Eugene. It was with regret that she advised him to seek someone else to marry—she did not want to become a burden to him in her later years. Having built up his hopes of marriage to Fannie, and Fannie's hopes, as well, Eugene was disheartened. Nevertheless, Fannie remained his customer, but he no longer came to the store.

A year or so later, Fannie heard that Eugene had married.

Chapter Six

*J*ust when the family returned to an almost predictable normality, another jolt intruded upon its somewhat tranquil existence. The health of Bella and Paul's only daughter seized the family with anguish and fear. Nora's symptoms sent her to the Children's Hospital. It was here that, after many tests, the doctors discovered the aching joints which pained the young child was a symptom of juvenile rheumatoid arthritis, known also as Still's Disease. Following extended months in the hospital, the doctors allowed her to leave, prescribing hot baths plus complete rest. The doctors also recommended a change of climate to alleviate her discomfort. Ideally, one possibility for relieving the pains of the seven-year old was to move her to the warm, dry, climate of Arizona. With the difference in the weather, there was a small chance the child would recover, and possibly even outgrow the debilitating disease. Or she could merely sustain residual symptoms, such as a slight deformity in her bones. Willing to sacrifice anything for her child's health, Bella made arrangements to move to Tucson, Arizona for a year's trial. She packed her bags and boarded the train westward with her ill youngster, leaving Paul behind.

Everyone in the family missed the young child and her mother, especially Bubba and Aunt Fannie. Paul, lonely without his family, tried to keep himself occupied in his business. He never took the time off to visit them. It was not feasible to close the business for an extended period of time since he needed the money to pay the mounting bills, nor was there any other person he could depend on to keep the store operating. Paul kept in constant touch with his wife and daughter. He continued his regular Sunday visits to Bubba's house while anxiously awaiting, with her and Aunt Fannie, for the day of Bella's and Nora's return.

The year stretched out. When Bella and Nora returned home after twelve months in the West, a remarkable change in Nora's physical condition had taken place. The youngster looked healthy and happy. Still it was too early to tell if evidence of the illness would linger as she grew older. Apprehension among the medical men prevailed, and the young girl was kept under the surveillance of her physicians.

The typical days of life returned slowly. Innocently the years moved ahead where winters jostled the springs, and the springs stirred the summers. Through this period of time Aunt Fannie, once past the grief of turning down the offer for her hand in marriage, unassumingly carried on her work.

Fannie's thriving business kept her days filled. She was proud of the productive life she led, earning a comfortable living despite her affliction. Naively, she thought it was the way of the world that everybody carried out their obligations to the utmost of their ability, and that all persons did exactly what was expected of them without complaint. The

54

modest living—financial and physical independence for which Fannie strived, and in which she found success—was a source of fulfillment to her. The war years had been good to store profits. The self-reliance and confidence gave her the inner security to which she had looked forward since entering the United States. One could say Fannie had developed into a career woman. In those days, though, they would call her a "business woman."

During the war Columbia Avenue had become rougher and a challenging area for business people. Originally the neighborhood had been a quiet, friendly place, but a change had taken place. Harry was still selling his speciality cuts of meat in the market, and he added fruits and vegetables for his customer's convenience. My uncle enjoyed the business and, being a friendly sort of individual, took the opportunity to chat with his customers. He worked in the the store until his son-in-law, Milton, who had joined him after returning from service, took over as the manager.

Though the meat market was still in operation, my parents tried to talk Fannie into moving her business to a different location—a safer one. Paul, too, was anxious to see his sister-in-law move to another area of the city, and into a larger store. Fannie, however, took it for granted she could cope with the changing scene. After all, she was deeply respected by her steady customers, many of whom referred to her as "Miss Fannie." As the children of her customers were growing up, even they continued to honor her with the title.

My aunt felt comfortable in that neighborhood after being in business for almost twenty years. Perhaps in her sincerity she thought that no hoodlum would harm an afflicted person. Too, knowing that Harry was close at hand should a problem arise gave her a false sense of security.

A few years back, a system had been wired between the butcher shop and Aunt Fannie's store in case of an emergency. If my aunt sensed herself in any danger, she could push a button under the counter and a bell would sound in Harry's store. Fannie was confident someone from the butcher shop would check on the urgency of the alarm within in a matter of seconds.

Thus, Fannie never considered changing locations. She hesitated as she thought about packing merchandise, moving it and setting up a new store, although she was sure members of her family would help her if she so decided. Familiar with the work that moving entails, since it had been only about three years prior that she and my grandmother moved into the house on Malvern Avenue, Fannie was reluctant to experience the same commotion, this time on a grander scale.

Before long, she found herself in the car on Sunday afternoons with Thomas and Paul, looking at prospective locations in various sections of the city. While they considered many possibilities, there were factors other than location to be weighed, one of them being accessibility to public transportation. Fannie's legs were not as strong as they had been twenty years before she had opened the store on Columbia Avenue. But Uncle Paul and my father insisted they had found the ideal location, only half a block from a bus stop. Fannie glanced around at the space which was to house her new place of business. The grandeur overwhelmed her. The area was wider and deeper than the building which presently accommodated her business, and Aunt Fannie wondered how she was going to manage walking the distance back and forth many times a day. She voiced a complaint to her brothers-in-law.

"It's too big, I don't need so much space."

"We'll bring in the carpenter to build shelves and a partition," came the reply.

With the help of her family Aunt Fannie rented the building on 60th Street, started to pack, and made arrangements to have the merchandise moved. Setting up a store with freshly-painted walls and appealing merchandise attracted numerous customers. She even bought some new items that she had never carried before. The location was a good choice, and Fannie hoped to develop the same relationship with her new clientele that she had had with her customers on Columbia Avenue.

High shelves and new counters presented the housewares attractively. The only problem was that my aunt now had to climb a six-foot ladder at least a half-dozen times a day to reach a boxed piece of merchandise that she had stocked on the upper shelves.

To Aunt Fannie's delight, my parents, who had since replaced their living room furniture, hauled an old wing chair to Fannie's store one Sunday.

"You did this for me?" she questioned in near disbelief, just as she always did whenever someone graciously presented her with a gift, or performed an act of kindness. Fannie was overcome with her sister's and brother-in-law's thoughtfulness to ease her tiring body. She was grateful to sit in the piece of furniture that had been theirs.

But she did not take time to rest. She always found something to do, never giving in to the difficulty behind her task. As an example, in anticipation of trash collection, my aunt would struggle to push a heavy carton of rubbish onto the sidewalk. It usually happened that either a passing customer, or another store owner, saw my aunt stooped over in her effort, and would come to the rescue. It amazed these friendly people, who got to know her habits well, that this dauntless woman took charge of her duties, hesitating to ask for help. Fannie insisted on doing things herself if it were at all humanly possible. She greeted challenges with resolution. Or was it a matter of exercising her independence?

At least there was a bathroom in the new store, which was an added convenience to my aunt's comforts. Still, since she was alone in the store most of the time, she had to lock the front store door whenever she had to use it.

Aunt Fannie checked orders and filled in stock. Members of the family insisted she hire a stock boy. After a lot of coaxing she did ask several of her customers if they knew a high school boy who was willing to work after school. As a last resort, my aunt employed a young man to do the tasks that she realized had become too strenuous for her.

Minnie helped Fannie with customers some weekends, and during sales (when they were on good speaking terms), and she would occasionally stop by just to keep her sister company. Bella was unable to find much time to spend with Aunt Fannie, being caught up catering to her husband and daughter both of whom demanded much of her attention.

Through my high school and college days I periodically trimmed the display windows for my aunt. It was also my job to print price signs with India ink on poster-board for counter displays. Aunt Fannie gave my parents a description of the signs she needed, with the affixed prices, over the telephone during the week, and on the following Sunday my parents delivered them to her. I was not allowed to accept payment for fulfilling my dutiful role. Being part of the family unit I was expected to carry out my obligations as such, and I carried them out willingly.

Exhausted by the end of the week, Fannie slept late each Sunday, her one day off. This was the day to pay the household bills and balance the checkbook. Sunday was the day, too, for catching up on newspapers and writing letters before her sisters and their families arrived in the mid-afternoon. Fannie corresponded with her mother's brother and her cousins in Russia. In her younger years my aunt had learned to read and write elementary Yiddish, the tongue spoken by the Jewish people in Eastern Europe. She explained to me once that, after losing contact with these relatives, the family in America wanted to know if they were still alive after World War II. At the urging of my grandmother who wanted to know if her brother was still alive, Fannie's uncle was located through HIAS when the war was over. Because letters were censored during Stalin's Communist regime, and particularly the ones addressed to apparent Jewish names on the envelopes, much of the mail had been confiscated and destroyed, never reaching its destination. Subsequently, a message was delivered from her brother in Russia reading: "Everybody is fine. Please do not try to contact us anymore."

Being Jews, their lives were in jeopardy. They would have been punished or, worse yet, killed if they received any information from the free world. Bubba was distraught to think she would never hear from her relatives again, but realized it was a warning. The writing ceased.

I remember how long it used to take Aunt Fannie to compose a letter. Although she wrote to relatives in Yiddish, her English improved remarkably, and her vocabulary grew steadily. Dependent on the dictionary for the correct spelling of words, my aunt became more adept at expressing herself in the language of her adopted country. Aunt Fannie showed me once, pulling from her handbag, a list of commonly-used words that she referred to when she wrote a letter. The list was handy when, at the store, she found a few minutes to start a message, and a dictionary was unavailable. While searching through her drawers I found numerous parcels of papers on which she had listed the spelling of numbers and other words. Aunt Fannie had even scrawled words in her address book for ready access!

Aunt Fannie wrote to her nephew Joe while he was in China and, along with other members of the family, showed her patriotism in many ways during the war. My aunt joined those Americans who invested in war bonds as a means of showing support for her country and gratitude for the opportunities democracy represented. When she bought the government bonds, she knew she was lending the United States money it sorely needed, and also envisioned the security the accrued interest would offer in the distant future.

Aware, too, of the critical need for blood in the theaters of war, Aunt Fannie was proud to become a donor on a regular

60

basis. She persisted in this benevolent act for many years beyond the end of the war. When anemia forced her to halt her contributions, she felt deprived of one of the most humane means of giving of herself. Aunt Fannie thought of the donation of blood as a source of strength from her own lifeline. For her it was something different, and something less, to simply write a check for a charitable cause. She did that often since she could not give of her time, or from her energy.

Rummaging through papers in the apartment, I noticed receipts that had accumulated from the many donations my aunt sent to charities over the years which she rarely refused, even if she sent a check for only one dollar. Her vulnerability to all varieties of appeals revealed itself as I flipped through a collection of more of them on the table. Holding a card in my hand naming her a member of the Automobile Association of America, I shook my head at her unsuspecting ways. She thought AAA was a charity. I grinned, mercifully, at the beneficent nature of my dear aunt for, of the four sisters, neither she nor my mother ever learned to drive.

Aunt Fannie's generosity extended beyond solicited charities. On the approach of a niece's or nephew's birthday, without fail, she would send a check. As usual, the card in which the gift was enclosed included a hand-written expression of sincere wishes in a tone distinctly that of her speech inflection. I could always hear her voice reading the personal greeting she wrote in conjunction with the printed words on the card. These same gifts were duplicated to relatives on holidays and anniversaries, and continued throughout the births of her great nieces and nephews.

In lieu of volunteering for fund-raising events, she donated money to the nearby synagogue. A religious woman, Fannie adhered to the *mitzvah* of giving, as taught in the ethics of Judaism: "the more a person gives the more he or she gets in return." Each year at Passover, upholding an old Jewish tradition, Aunt Fannie, sent a check to the rabbi of the synagogue of which she was a member. A tradition, the gift was to ensure the spiritual leader sufficient money to buy matzos, the unleavened bread eaten at this season. With this act of *Tzedakah*, the giving of charity, Fannie included a touching note in a most carefully written script. She took pleasure in giving whatever she could, whenever she could.

This kindhearted woman kept a firm eye on her accounts and learned to handle her hard-earned money wisely. My aunt spent neither foolishly nor needlessly for herself, yet gave unbegrudgingly and sincerely. Fannie gave so much to others and took so little for herself.

One of her few pleasures, too, were the open-air concerts given free by the city, just a short trolley ride from her house. It drew her like a magnet even though the distance of the walk from the trolley stop to the benches in the park was exerting after a long day on her feet. There was no Victrola in the house to hear strains of wonderful melodies and harmonies which she loved. Listening to the orchestral music, relaxing outdoors in the warm summer evenings, gave my aunt the opportunity to see some of the famous conductors and soloists perform.

Sometimes I would accompany my aunt to the concerts and stay overnight at Bubba's house. Since both Aunt Fannie and I appreciated the arts, and she would not think of traveling into town to buy a ticket for herself, I once purchased tickets to attend the theater together. Counting on it being a treat for both of us, I chose a play. As a teenager, I was unaware of the story even though I had known the book from which the play was adapted was a best seller. The name of the play was "Tobacco Road." As the show progressed, I grew more and more restless. I slid down in my seat, embarrassed at exposing my aunt to such bawdy language. Had I only known! I am certain my aunt understood the words and context of the story, but I am also certain she had never spoken any such words in English—in any language for that matter—and she spoke several languages. Although she uttered not a word during the performance, I felt the tension of the silence.

PART III

MALVERN AVENUE

Chapter Seven

*D*espite her physical image, Fannie looked like a typical working woman. She dressed neatly, always with a necklace that matched her dress, and small bows that graced her hair.

Oxfords with a built-in lift designed for her right foot were the only shoes Fannie knew. She purchased two colors, black and brown, to maintain some style in matching her dresses, of which there were few varieties.

A fur coat was one of the rare luxuries my aunt allowed herself, only at the persuasion of Gertie and Minnie, who each had one. The fur was purchased for the sake of keeping Fannie warm while she walked in the center of town in the winter, but she also felt like a princess wrapped in the gray ringlets. My aunt wore it, also, on special occasions, which were infrequent, and carried herself with pride.

The Philadelphia "Center City" stores were open late on Wednesday evenings, but the store on 60th Street closed an hour or so earlier that day. The early closing gave my aunt an opportunity to catch a bus going downtown to make some purchases for herself and her mother. My aunt learned to find her way alone by public transportation to places she wanted to go.

The evening in town gave Fannie the opportunity to have her hair shampooed and set, and nails manicured and polished, luxuries she deemed a necessity. No one could guess when the gray strands of hair began to appear, for the auburn-tinted color lent Fannie self-confidence from her waist upward.

About once every six months, my aunt ordered prescription shoes to accommodate her walking. Fannie's shoe wore out quickly, and became scuffed easily since the foot of her lame leg did not rise far from the ground. Aunt Fannie's legs, fatigued from the day's work slowed her gait, and many errands had to wait until the following Wednesday evening.

When I came home from the Army in 1952, after the Korean War, I noticed age was creeping up on Aunt Fannie. The energy she once possessed diminished while the left leg that carried the weight of her body began to grow weaker. Walking the length of the store to wait on customers, and fill in stock with incoming orders exhausted the uncomplaining woman. A mistress to her determination of never becoming a burden for as long as she was humanly capable unceasingly remained in the back of her mind.

And yet, Fannie made demands upon her family. She came to expect people to wait on her, which included her two younger sisters and their husbands and, later, their children.

Bubba repeated over and over to Bella and Minnie, "When I'm gone, take good care of Fannie." However, Bubba did not tell this to Gertie. Her eldest daughter was not well, and in her later years was always in and out of the hospital. In addition to her heart condition, Gertie had developed diabetes. She was placed on a carefully measured diet which slimmed the majestic-looking woman to a smaller figure, though an imposing height continued to be her adorning feature. Episodes of congestive heart failure put her in bed for days at a time.

Often when my mother was confined in her room, she insisted my father not tell anyone that she was sick. My father covered up for her more times than I can count by not telling any of my aunts, or my grandmother, that his wife lay ill in bed. Gertie perceived her mother and sisters, who assumed a grim outlook when it came to circumstances they could not control, to be highly emotional women. The family never suspected how many times the doctor came to the house, nor the numerous days she lay in bed drugged by the injections to rest her weakened heart.

Although Gertie worked in the store between sieges of illness, Thomas, at least, was able to maintain regular business hours while his wife lay in bed in the apartment above. My father sat in the second floor apartment, his two hands folded under his chin in worriment of his beloved wife until the downstairs bell announcing a customer interrupted his darkest thoughts.

Joe, who graduated as a medical doctor after he returned from the service, was assured our mother was under good medical care, having stayed in contact with Gertie's physicians even though he now lived in Connecticut. When he lived in Philadelphia during his internship he had assumed the role of medical advisor to the family, always available for opinions and advice. Everyone was proud of him, and rightly so, since he was the first grandchild to become a professional. The family respected what he had to say without question. Where the sisters allowed their emotions to rule, Joe was able to change an aunt's perspective, interspersing emotions with hope and a bit of humor.

Through these years, the family expanded to a next generation, and was still meeting at Bubba's house for most of the Sundays in the year. By now Rosalie, in spite of her chronic disease, had given birth to a boy, and a few years later, a girl. She and Milton lived in the suburbs within the family circle. Rosalie was able to push the baby carriage within a short distance from her home to visit her mother or Bubba in the middle of the week.

I had married while in the service, and a few years later Jeannine and I also had a girl and boy of our own. Meanwhile Millie had moved to Ohio. However, when her marriage ended in divorce while she was pregnant with her third child, she moved back to Philadelphia. Nora was still living at home with her parents, working at odd jobs and continuing her education.

Bubba looked forward to seeing her great-grandchildren and watching them grow. She was proud of the legacy she would leave. As the Sunday ritual prevailed, Bubba no longer cooked the big meals she once did, and the card-playing came to a halt. The families were increasing, and Bubba was aging.

My grandmother began having problems with her stomach. Frequent visits to the doctor indicated she was getting no better. After seeing her in his office a few times, realizing the medication he prescribed was not helping, the doctor admitted Bubba to the hospital for a battery of tests. It seemed to us, the grandchildren, that our Bubba was there for weeks and weeks. The conversations for the ears of the younger generation were hushed, and although I surmise that my aunts knew the diagnosis, the critical news was withheld from us. It was obvious that Bubba was not improving.

I remember the stories Aunt Fannie used to tell of how hard Bubba worked to keep her daughters together and fed in Russia. How she kept house for them here in the new land and coped with a strange-sounding language. How she spoke only Yiddish to my mother and my aunts, and to her grandchildren who understood her native tongue better than she understood the language of her new country. How quiet was my grandmother's voice, barely rising above a murmur when she gave her sage advice.

My memory takes me back to her funeral. I remember the wailing of her daughters. I recall hearing Fannie's voice—how the vibrations trembled through the deafened air. Fannie was crying for her mother; more so she was crying for herself.

Chapter Eight

*B*ubba's death bound the sisters to each other for the time being. As in the past, it was the tragedies that kept the family together. It was tragedies the four sisters seemed to thrive on. Now that both parents were dead, they wept together in their mourning. Their bitter youth in Russia and the bountiful years in America hugged their memories.

Fannie was alone now. Her sisters had their own families to take care of. Aunt Fannie looked upon her mother's role with wonderment. Her mind dwelt on the angelic woman who was an inspiration, and Fannie vowed to continue following the moral teachings her mother had instilled in her. She remembered that Bubba had taught her to make the best of things, and Fannie grasped this advice, which gave her courage relative to her "condition." Now that she was alone, she cogitated on how well she could live out the remainder of her years in remembrance of her mother's maxims.

Although my aunt knew how to manage well in the business world, Aunt Fannie had little knowledge of the mundane tasks necessary for survival. Because of her long days at the business, Fannie was never expected to share in the housework, and held no responsibilities at home with the exception of paying the household expenses. Her mother always prepared meals for her. In fact, on Saturdays when my grandmother was younger, she traveled on the trolleys, carrying Fannie's lunch to the Columbia Avenue store. Bubba stayed then with my aunt until Uncle Harry drove both her and Aunt Fannie home when the store closed.

Since my grandmother had shielded Fannie and catered to her daughter's needs for most of her life, my aunt found herself virtually helpless in managing the house. When they married, Bella and Minnie learned household efficiency out of necessity, but Fannie had not been prepared for this phase of life when she would have to clean house and cook for herself. Struggling for independence for most of her life, it now behooved Fannie to rely on her sisters. Being ignorant of many essential tasks in a home, she was pleased when Bella and Minnie offered their assistance to help her organize the many household chores. It was a blessing that her sisters looked after her—just as Bubba had implored them to do before she died.

When Bubba was ill, Minnie had cooked for my grandmother and Fannie. She had prepared the meals at her house and carried the warm food to Bubba's, knowing Fannie was incapable of putting a meal together, and had neither the time nor energy to learn at such a critical time. During this emergency, Minnie also took on the responsibility of laundering the soiled bed clothes at her house during Bubba's suffering. She walked the few blocks that separated their houses, hauling the linens back and forth to her mother's house in a woven basket clutched between her two hands. She did it graciously as a dutiful daughter and sister.

Each sister brought Fannie cooked meals for the first few weeks after Bubba died, but eventually Fannie was forced to learn to cook. Both Bella and Minnie rendered suggestions on how to prepare certain foods while Bella shopped for most of the groceries. Fannie reimbursed her sister for the food bills, for Fannie expected nothing that was not rightfully hers.

Fannie carried on the tradition of eating kosher meat, just as when her mother was alive. My grandmother kept a kosher kitchen, in which dairy and meat dishes are cooked and eaten separately, and she used only kosher food supplies, customs which Aunt Fannie followed. Despite the fact that Harry owned a meat market, my aunt ordered meats and poultry from the same butcher her mother had bought from once a week.

Within a few months, Aunt Fannie was able to cook a meal for herself. Every night when she came home from work she prepared dinner for herself, cooking and eating well into the late evening. When she was finished, she stood at the sink, washing and drying the dishes, no matter how tired she was.

Although Fannie was weary at the end of the week, she could no longer afford the luxury of sleeping late on Sunday mornings. Routinely, on her one day away from the store, my aunt cleaned the house and washed some laundry. Climbing down the almost-vertical steps to the basement under the dim light, Fannie soaped and rinsed her personal garments by hand. Then she hung the wet clothing on lines strung amidst the pipes in the basement to dry overnight. Arriving home from work the next day, my aunt climbed down the steps after dinner to remove the laundry, and then carried it up two flights of steps into the bedroom.

Changing bed sheets was especially challenging for Fannie. Because of her short stature, and the loss of muscular strength in the one leg, Fannie found it difficult to lean across the three-quarter size bed that stood against the wall to adjust the broad expanse of fabric without jostling her leg. Since Bella and Minnie had done their share to help her until now, Fannie persevered at this bedmaking chore alone. It was a matter of self-reliance that stood in the way of her asking a sister to help with this task, even though it was Bella who now took the used linens home to wash in her machine every few weeks.

The petty arguments that still often arose, though not as frequent, were quickly glossed over. Each sister, for the present, had a common purpose in looking after Fannie—stubborn as she was at times.

I am sure Bella and Minnie responded to Aunt Fannie's needs in respect to my grandmother's wish. But somehow, Fannie did not agree with Bella and Minnie's ideas in certain aspects of maintaining a house nearly as often as she agreed with Gertie. It was her eldest sister whose advice Fannie heeded the most. The current calm conditions between the sisters were slated to worsen.

Fannie gradually grew accustomed to doing her household tasks on Sunday. It became easier for her as time went on. She worked as swiftly as her legs would carry her, and left some tasks undone, for in the early afternoon, she wanted to be ready in time for one of her sisters and a brother-in-law to take her to *Horn & Hardart*, a popular restaurant nearby. Here they enjoyed their big meal of the day, sitting and relaxing together in the middle of a Sunday afternoon.

My parents usually were the family members who took "Fanya," as my mother lovingly called her sister in her Russian name, to dinner resuming their weekly visits when my mother felt well enough. Often Jeannine and I would take our children to visit with Fannie for a few hours on a Sunday and join my parents and Aunt Fannie for dinner at the restaurant.

My mother often brought food she had cooked to tide my aunt over for a few days. With a great admiration for her eldest sister and her husband, Fannie welcomed the opportunity to speak with Gertie and Thomas in person, to discuss some of the problems she did not want to talk about on the telephone.

After Bubba's death, it became increasingly more difficult for Fannie to walk. The years were moving faster while my aunt's pace was slowing due to the weakened bones of her right hip. This physical problem often caused Fannie to lose her balance. She was unable to grab onto a piece of furniture some of the time, and one Sunday while she was cleaning in a hurry, Fannie slipped and fell. When this happened before, as it had on many occasions, she picked herself up and went on with her duties. But this time my aunt lay still on the floor for many minutes, stunned! Many minutes later, after gaining her composure, Fannie noticed the telephone a few feet away and she, little by little, "wiggled my body across the living room floor to dial Minnie's number." By now the leg which had given her so much physical and mental anguish had become swollen. Fannie needed to be taken to the hospital as soon as possible to discover, through examination, if any physical damage had occurred.

When Fannie arrived at the emergency room in the hospital, the doctors ordered X-rays. A view of the picture showed a fracture in the bone of her leg. The doctor set Fannie's leg in a cast and detained her in the hospital. My aunt was very unhappy. She intensely disliked being a patient and could not wait to be discharged after a week. During this time she was taught to walk on crutches, after which she was sent home to recuperate.

My aunt stayed alone in the house—at her own insistence—resting in her upstairs bedroom, under the care of her two younger sisters. Minnie and Bella visited often bringing her hot meals, making sure Fannie ate three meals a day.

Aunt Fannie got used to hobbling around upstairs on crutches, rather well, in fact. Having stayed on the second floor for a few weeks—much too long for Fannie—she was elated when the doctor gave her permission to slide down the steps on her buttocks, but only once a day. She knew that her progress would alleviate some dependence upon her sisters. She loathed the feeling of helplessness.

Now that my aunt was downstairs during the day, and healing well, friends and neighbors came to visit with her. It was a windy day in autumn when the front door bell rang. Fannie, sitting on the living room sofa, was resting her broken leg on a hassock. My aunt feared, as usual, that if she did not answer the door quickly enough by the time she stood up and positioned her crutches, the person waiting at the door would turn and leave. In her haste to unlock and open the front door, Fannie tripped. She landed on the floor once more. It was again necessary for her to be driven to the hospital emergency room, and as before, there were more examinations and x-rays. This time she had broken her wrist. With a leg encased in plaster, and a cast covering her arm and part of her hand, Aunt Fannie was sent home. The recuperation period had just been extended. The store was closed for almost two months, and no money was coming in.

Prior to Fannie's second fall, Minnie and Harry had made plans to go to Florida for a month, just as they did every winter. Harry had worked long hours in his business. He had earned the vacation. Minnie thought it was not necessary to stay home to care for her sister. She had done so much for her until now, and believed she owed it to her husband to enjoy time together. Going ahead with their plans, they left Fannie under the care of Bella.

Weeks passed, and Fannie improved. She moved through the apartment now caring for herself, though with less ease and more caution. The cast was finally removed from her leg. Without waiting until her wrist healed completely, Fannie went back to work in the store, a cast on her arm. Happy to see her, my aunt's customers were shocked to hear of the double accidents.

As the months lingered and winter arrived, Fannie's bones finally healed, though my aunt's general tempo slowed considerably. The broken bones had not helped the vigor and enthusiasm she once possessed. The days stretched before her and long before store closing, she was more tired each day. Cooking meals at the end of the day was a chore, and by nightfall the steps to the second floor bedroom seemed to grow in number.

Seeing that Fannie's legs were losing their strength, particularly after the fall, and that her walking became increasingly labored, the family suggested she convert the house into a duplex—an apartment on each floor. The transition to living on the lower floor, not having to walk steps, would be easier for Fannie, except for the steep steps to the front porch of the house.

Fannie planned to rent the upstairs apartment and have someone else, at least, live in the same building. The rent, too, would add supplemental income which, within a few years, would pay for the alterations. The extra bedrooms sat untouched upstairs, and the clothing and collected things that filled the closets could be condensed, or given away.

The dining room on the first floor, where the family ate Bubba's cooking every Sunday, was not being utilized. The extra furniture in each of the rooms only meant added cleaning for Aunt Fannie who already had enough work to keep her busy for one day. To make life more comfortable for herself—knowing her walking problems would worsen in a matter of time—Fannie welcomed the recommendation without hesitation and the usual coaxing. Previous minor slips on the steps and broken limbs from falling were enough to convince Fannie she was ready for a one floor dwelling—as long as she remained in the same structure in which her beloved mother had spent the last years of her life. Fannie gave the word to go ahead and contract the job.

Even though her sisters had offered many unsolicited recommendations in the past. Fannie had not always been receptive to their ways of thinking. This, however, was an exceptional time when all of the family members agreed that it was a splendid idea. Minnie helped, and Bella helped. Together the three of them decided what furniture Fannie no longer needed. The extra pieces were sold, and after the renovations Fannie moved downstairs into a comfortable three-room apartment. Having the conveniences she needed on one floor simplified life for Aunt Fannie. She did not miss the trudge to the upstairs bedroom at the end of the day. The steps from the curb of the street to the porch of the dwelling somehow seemed to have gotten steeper through the years.

With the help of a real estate agent, the newly designed apartment above Aunt Fannie's was rented to an elderly woman. It was not the ideal situation my aunt had anticipated. The woman was noisy night and day, though Fannie persevered with the circumstances and said nothing to her. She was content the rooms were occupied.

It wasn't until six years later that the tenant moved. The apartment stood unoccupied for a year. When my aunt heard that her niece Nora was looking for a place to live after graduating from college, she suggested the young girl rent the second floor apartment. Even so, Fannie could not understand why young people wanted to leave the security of family life as long as they are single. For her, it was difficult to comprehend this new "liberation" of women.

But Nora intensely disapproved of the idea. Truthfully, it would not have been a good arrangement for either of them. Nora and Aunt Fannie each had strong, distinct personalities. Knowing Fannie, she would have felt compelled to act as a surrogate mother to her niece. Consequently, Nora would have rebelled in her effort to exercise her direction of thinking. The attachment would have caused Fannie unnecessary anxiety, and the clear-cut differences that were bound to arise would have formulate a permanent bitterness between them.

After Aunt Fannie gave up hopes of renting to Nora, the long-empty apartment was once again leased to another tenant who was just as noisy as the former one. The loud radio proved too much to tolerate; music vibrated through the walls when my aunt came home tired from a long day's work. She told the real estate agent not to renew the man's lease. Fannie found it a nuisance to contend with an inconsiderate person, despite that the tenant paid his rent on time. And so it went for quite a while. It was not easy for the agent to find a suitable tenant for a long period of time.

Chapter Nine

*T*he freedom of worshipping in a country free of the fear of being shot at in cold blood, had a profound influence on both my grandmother and my aunt. Throughout the years Fannie had become absorbed in religion; religious ideals became her way of life. Though she worked on the Sabbath, my aunt found time to read and study the Bible. She made every attempt to live by its teachings, basing her principles of everyday living on the Ten Commandments and the teachings of the Old Testament.

When Bubba and Aunt Fannie lived on Poplar Street, they walked to the nearby synagogue on the High Holidays, and occasionally attended Sabbath services. They saw Joe and me, at age thirteen, celebrate our admittance to Jewish manhood at that very synagogue where they worshipped. We had prepared for the religious ceremony in Philadelphia with the rabbi from that congregation. On these very special days my aunt closed the store especially to attend services. The celebrations were much more important to her than losing a day's income.

My aunt sensed a righteous life would bring its own rewards, and after the death of her mother she clung to religion ever more so in her everyday thoughts and in her work. For one thing, Fannie assumed that abiding by the tenets of the Bible would protect her from the increasing crime taking place in the city streets. She tried hard to believe that no one would infringe upon a crippled person. To be lame was suffering enough. But she was mistaken.

Late one afternoon two men Aunt Fannie thought to be prospective customers, walked into the 60th Street store. As Fannie walked toward them, the man with a wide grin crossing his face asked for a specific item. In the meantime, the accompanying male seemingly looked at some specialty near the front counter. While Fannie's attention was focused on showing the first man the merchandise he had asked for, the accomplice adroitly stepped behind the counter, opened the cash register and put all the dollar bills into his pocket. The two men ran out of the store so quickly that the speed of the scene left Fannie both dazed and frightened. Fannie was quick to resume her composure and hurried to the front of the store. She locked the door, then picked up the telephone to call the police.

Fannie had trusted people until now. Her belief in the honesty and integrity of human beings festered after the encounter with these devious persons. When in business on Columbia Avenue, she felt protected by the proximity to her brother-in-law's market and the bell wired to Harry's store. Here at the present location, my aunt was more or less isolated from people who had a genuine concern for her welfare. Yes, there were businessmen on the same block with whom Aunt Fannie was acquainted. In fact, a kind, concerned storekeeper across the street often drove my aunt home in inclement weather, traveling a few miles out of his way to accommodate her.

When things calmed down, and she gave the incident some thought, Fannie was comforted in that it was only the money the men wanted and nothing more. She knew that she was still capable of making up the lost cash with future sales. The financial loss was nothing compared to having been bodily injured.

Aunt Fannie could not conceive that times were changing; people were changing. Television and the nuclear age were altering attitudes. A drug-ridden society was beginning to surface. Although my aunt listened to the news and read a great deal, she was somewhat sheltered in her world, protected by the past, oblivious to the present. She remembered when people trusted their neighbors and left their doors unlocked, when the greater part of the population in this country respected another person's property. Fannie would shake her head in disbelief.

Through her spirituality, which had yet to be undermined, Aunt Fannie expressed contentment with the possessions she toiled so hard to acquire and retain—adequate food, clothing to keep her body warm, and her own home. She was ever grateful to have retained physiological health up until now, and that she possessed the intelligence to own and operate a business. Just to be able to get up out of bed and go to work each day gave my aunt ultimate satisfaction.

Fannie was a modest person. A woman of frugality, she lived in her measured ways, having learned to make things suffice with the little that was available in Russia. In fact she knew no other course. And how well she remembered the stock market crash of 1929, the year after the store opened, when money was scarce and her family had become used to what then were the finer things of life.

Aunt Fannie was everlastingly thankful she no longer suffered the starvation she knew in Russia as a child. Her wardrobe was minimal, for she bought only the apparel necessary to look well groomed, hardly thinking in terms of fashion. And the homes in which she had lived, where the roofs never leaked, were warm in the winters. She was happy to have a place to sit, and a bed to lie in despite that the furniture looked worn and faded. These simple pleasures granted Aunt Fannie the inner peace she sought.

And so it was perplexing for my unsophisticated aunt to comprehend the younger generation. Having all of the basic comforts they needed, they still wanted more— even at the risk of stealing.

Aware now of societal changes, yet not conscious of its over-reaching effects, Fannie continued to work in the store. She was thankful she had not been harmed, and prayed that there would be no reoccurrence of the same scene.

Complacency settled in with her unchanging routine— but not for long. A few months after the robbery, when there was no one else in the store but Fannie, a similar plot took place. Again she escaped unscathed. It was only the money the robbers wanted. The affirmation that a power greater than hers was watching over Fannie took a firmer hold within her devout thinking.

Only strong faith and determination helped Fannie keep the store open. Despite her increased fear, she had no intention of closing the business. After all, this had been her life's work. Devotion to her customers, and keeping herself occupied, were her main objectives. Each day she looked forward to going to the store and greeting the people who kept her in business. For all of these years she knew nothing else.

But Fannie's safety was in jeopardy. The whole family worried that luck at the 60th Street store was running out. Alone in the store but for the few customers that came in at a time, and not being able to protect herself very well, Aunt Fannie was an easy mark.

Chapter Ten

*D*uring her thirty years or longer as a shopkeeper, Fannie became more than exclusively a business woman and landlady. Having bought the building which housed her second store, my aunt became a property owner of a building other than the house she owned. Above the first floor were two apartments rented to tenants. The former frightened Russian immigrant who limped toward the officials at Ellis Island, terrified of being deported to her original homeland, carried out her daily duties and succeeded far beyond what she could have ever fantasized in her deprived youth. But praise her with her accomplishments and a delicate body would shrink into the oversized chair, a smile appearing on her face which read, "I did what I could. I am no different from anybody else who tried to make a living. I did my best."

She felt blessed that she was able, for all of those years, to move her paralyzed leg without the assistance of a cane, or a walker. For a few years now, the gnawing threat hung over her as an ominous cloud: the unrelenting thought that her legs would not carry her any longer—she would not be able to walk, not even with the support of a cane—that she would have to spend the last part of her life in a wheelchair. Through her tenacity, until now, all of her prayers were answered. The challenges my aunt overcame during her entire lifetime, ironically, created within her a spirit that would have discouraged a lesser-determined woman. A personal bargain, and a bargain with her intimate God—not to become a burden to another person, including herself—provided Aunt Fannie with uncommon perseverance. She would not give up, nor would she give in.

Since the days of her escape from Russia, Fannie always believed a divine power kept a constant watch over her. Fannie's religious faith grew while the strength of her legs weakened. The strain of the extra weight on the good leg was beginning to have its effect as the pain from arthritis surged through her hip. With the accumulation of years, and increasing incapacity, Aunt Fannie believed it was her good fortune that she was able to earn a living. Her financial independence was guaranteed from the day she opened her first store.

When my aunt talked about her life, she credited success to moral support and sage advice from her family. The family as an important nucleus was the crux of many of her discourses. Our conversations frequently included an examination of the strength in the family structure as a unit, and her face would light up whenever I told her Jeannine and I were planning to attend a family function on my wife's side of the family. She was unyielding in her belief of family unity despite friction that consistently interrupted the harmony between her sisters and herself—in spite of the persistent independence she exhibited throughout the years.

Looking back over the past, I believe Bella and Minnie's attitudes had changed. The two sisters sincerely held Fannie's best interest at heart—and particularly after the robberies—when they pressed her to give up the store, that she had worked enough years to earn retirement. It was time for her to stay home and rest. They saw her legs giving way, that Fannie had a problem standing on her feet for most of the day. They knew the effort it took for her to get dressed in the mornings, eat breakfast, and go to work. And they knew how hard it was for Fannie to do trivial tasks for herself after work each night, and how tired she was on Sundays. Workdays sapped her strength and slowed her walking more so even though the stubbornness of Fannie's will kept her body in motion.

Even my mother, to whom my aunt looked for counsel and reassurance, could not persuade Fannie to stop working. Gertie, whose health was failing, had inspired Aunt Fannie. My aunt rationalized that as long as Gertie could manage to wait on customers without giving in to her maladies, there was no reason why Fannie could not find the stamina to continue to work in her business. After all, she had no debilitating disease such as diabetes, and her legs still carried her where she wanted to go, though in a slackening motion.

"What am I going to do?" Fannie questioned in defense. "How am I going to make a living?"

My aunt dwelled on how her customers, who depended on her line of merchandise, the fair prices, and the extra considerations she offered, would miss her. She was more concerned about her clients than her depleted energy sapping her strength. Even following another robbery, Fannie clung to this stubborn attitude.

A man came into the store pretending he wanted to buy a gift. Fannie smiled, as usual, as she approached the customer while asking if she could help him. Instantly, the towering stranger whipped out a rope, quickly tying my aunt's wrists together, the palms of her hands facing each other. He grabbed her arm forcing her to walk to the back of the store. Fannie was stricken with panic. The man then shoved her into the rear, small bathroom while her heart raced. Her breathing was rapid, yet shallow. She tried to catch her breath. This was the second time in Fannie's life that overwhelming terror sneaked into every bone of her body. She feared the man was going to rape her. My aunt screamed to her assailant to take anything he wanted from the store, but not from her person. She pleaded with the aggressor not to harm her. The man slammed the door to the bathroom shut, grabbed the money from the cash register, and hastily left.

Fannie quietly listened through the door. When she was very sure she no longer heard noises, she worked at loosening the rope from her wrists and finally freed herself. She aimed herself toward the telephone and dialed Harry's number. Immediately, from the quivering, breathless sound of her voice, her brother-in-law detected that she was in danger. By the time Harry arrived and called the police, the robber was nowhere to be found. He was never caught.

Fannie spent a restless night. It was one more time Fannie was thankful she had not been physically violated. It was one more confirmation that the divine Being was looking after her. My aunt was assured He would continue to watch over her for the rest of her life.

The next morning Fannie discovered her body was covered with bruises. The scene intermittingly flashed through her mind for the rest of the day—and many days and nights thereafter.

The store stayed open for business, but Fannie remained cautious. The front door was always locked. Customers tapped on the front glass to get into the store, and each time Aunt Fannie walked haltingly to the front, turned the key and opened the door, allowing only patrons she recognized to enter.

Since the additional robbery, her sisters redoubled their efforts to persuade Fannie to close the business. They did all they could to convince her the time for retirement had, at last, come. Even her best friend, Sonia, hearing of the latest, and most threatening assault, joined the chorus: "Enough is enough," she begged. "Why wait until something worse happens? Don't take any more chances."

Considering everyone's repeated concern about her safety over the past six months, Fannie heeded their advice and made up her mind to finally retire. Plans for a closing sale were announced, and her lengthy career ended.

As she thought about the future, my aunt remarked, "I will surely miss all of my customers."

PART IV

RETIREMENT

Chapter Eleven

*I*t did not take long for Fannie to adjust to staying home once she resigned herself to the situation. There was enough work in the small apartment to keep her occupied. And there was more time for her to talk to her friends on the telephone. No longer did she have to say a quick goodbye and hang up the phone as she used to whenever a customer entered the store.

Soon the days fell into a system as habit fell into a routine. Cooking, cleaning, and taking care of the laundry each found its own day. Since for many years she cooked after coming home from work daily, my aunt submitted to a sensible suggestion. Gertie told Fannie it would be more efficient to cook her meals for the entire week on one day, package the food in portions, and place it into the freezer compartment of the refrigerator. At mealtime she had only to heat the serving, then rinse the few dishes she used each day. Fannie reveled in the idea, following the recommendation until the day, years later, when she entered the hospital.

Aunt Fannie never learned how to use the broiler inside the stove, nor did she ever learn to bake. She lived on the memories of her mother's tasty pastries—the apple strudel and potato knishes—but never ventured to bake them for herself.

Thursday was the prescribed day for preparing meals, the day when the aroma of meat and vegetables filled the small apartment. Because Fannie knew Gertie was not permitted to add salt to her diet due to her heart condition, she thought it wise to eliminate the seasoning for the sake of her own health. She learned to make chicken soup for the Sabbath, a dish that lasted for several meals. In the summertime, through the open windows, neighbors knew the day of the week by the smell as the odors drifted to the outdoor air. They knew Fannie was busy in the kitchen cooking, a flowered apron tied around her waist.

Bella continued to do the supermarket shopping for Fannie. When she could not spare the time, as occasionally happened, Fannie called on another family member to pick up a few things for her. If she knew that I, or my cousin, was coming to see her, she would request that we stop at the store to buy whatever it was she needed. We rarely declined her wishes.

Aunt Fannie liked to know ahead of time when someone was planning to visit her. She never relished interruptions from her schedule when she lived on Malvern Avenue. She wanted the chance to change from her work clothes into a clean, fresh garment, apply some lipstick and place a bow in her hair. She always took pride in her appearance and dressed neatly.

Self-discipline led my aunt to the keeping of the Sabbath, a practice she had been unable to uphold while in business. Fannie was able to rest from her work on Saturdays now that she was retired. For most of the morning she sat on the sofa reading a prayer book. The day also gave her the opportunity to catch up on reading: periodicals, books and reviewing the mail. It was the day, too, when she could take time to listen to the Metropolitan Opera broadcast over the radio, a special pleasure for her.

Now that she no longer worked, Fannie wanted to become an active part of the synagogue. It was a chance for her to get out of the house and see other people, to offset the loneliness she experienced since Bubba had died and since she had retired. Conversations with the congregants of all ages afforded her joy as she looked forward to meeting new friends and greeting old ones. She joined a group of women and became a student of the Bible. Fannie also became a member of the Sisterhood, and when she felt up to it, or when someone stopped by to drive her, she attended services on Friday nights or Saturday mornings.

A hat atop her tilted head, this woman who looked so fragile sat in an assigned seat at High Holiday services. Between the long services, during breaks, many of the women took short walks, except for Fannie. She knew she could not keep the fast pace of the other women and she stayed at her designated place, standing up and looking around. While Fannie stretched her legs, the rabbi's wife hurried back to sit with her friend. The two of them spent time together before the prayers started once again. The breaks were a convenient time for my aunt to *yenta*, talking about everybody and everything, the bantering bringing smiles to the faces of both women.

Pride stood in the way of Fannie asking someone for a ride to and from the the synagogue. When my grandmother was alive—my aunt younger, her legs more stable—the two of them walked to the house of prayer together. Even for a few years after Bubba died Fannie, slow of pace and strong of determination, attempted the three-block-long stretch to the synagogue. She was usually offered a ride home by one of the congregants. Someone was always willing to drive her, though infrequently, one of those well-meaning persons forgot his/her promise and departed without my aunt. Fannie felt a great disappointment in being left behind. "You always have a ride with us," assured the rabbi and his wife who had moved to another part of the city, "because we are going to the synagogue and coming back from there, so don't worry." Fannie was content knowing that somebody cared.

On the Day of Atonement each year, my aunt observed the ritual of fasting. Aside from the purpose of cleansing one's soul, as stated in the Torah, during this Holy Day, an empty stomach to Fannie served as a reminder of the days in Russia when there was very little food. The deprivation of nourishment beckoned my sensitive aunt to empathize with the people throughout the world who feel pangs of hunger every day.

Yom Kippur is the day, too, when inspirational prayers are said for the living and memorial prayers are read for the dead. Fannie had no premonition during that holiday in the autumn of her retirement in 1963, come Yom Kippur of the following year, she would be saying a memorial prayer for her sister Gertie.

Between my mother's condition—congestive heart failure and the diabetes—the doctor could not imagine what miracle was keeping my mother alive except for the will to survive. Eventually, the medication she had taken for many years was no longer as effective, and the spans between her symptomatic heart spasms grew shorter and shorter. On a cold day in January, Gertie became ill for the last time. Her lungs were filled with too much fluid, her heart could no longer stand the strain. Her organs had weakened to the point of collapse. Suddenly my Mom was gone.

Fannie standing next to Gertie.

Death to Fannie meant finality. And it was Gertie's death that brought back memories of Bubba, for the two of them had played similar roles in the life of my aunt. A mother gives birth to a child, feeds it, nurtures it, and teaches the

97

child right from wrong. Fannie's mother guided her limping daughter from childhood into maturity, looking forward to her daughter becoming a worthy, productive person, when she grew to adulthood. The tears that rolled from Fannie's eyes were tears for her elder sister, a sister who acted more like a mother to Fannie, for of all the sisters, Gertie was the one for whom Fannie cared the most.Gertie was her protector—the only person other than her mother who gave Fannie the courage and foresight to build an independent force within herself.

It was Gertie who reveled in the success of her lame younger sister, perceiving not her physical disability but her active and intelligent mind. Gertie was an understanding friend with whom Aunt Fannie shared secrets, hopes, and dreams—and little tales. Fannie felt the blow deeply. She remembered the many years Gertie had been sick, and knew that no human lives forever. The death of her sister made Fannie come to grips with her own mortality. Amidst her grief, my aunt felt a stronger need of faith than ever before, the urge to cling to a constancy that was her very own, something that would render her courage to face whatever the future held.

Now that the peacemaker in the family was gone, it was a struggle for Fannie to maintain a calm with Bella and Minnie.

Harsh words between the sisters were uttered more frequently. Being of a sensitive nature, Fannie was easily hurt by her sisters' innuendoes; the vocalized stings were periodically magnified. Rarely was there a serene interval when all three of the sisters were on speaking terms. The angles of the triangle were constantly shifting. Always, one was oblique.

98

Although my brother Joe had once been the person to whom the family turned concerning their problems, distance had minimized his contact with them since Joe and his family were living in New England where my brother had opened a medical practice. No longer was he sought for his objectivity toward my aunt's predicaments, as before. At the present, he was consulted only for his medical advice.

Therefore it was I, as my mother's successor, who became the mediator. I did not attempt to resolve the problems that arose between my aunts but rather acted as a sounding board for their skirmishes that originated from jealousy and pride.

Many were the times one aunt called me on the telephone to complain about another aunt. Within the week, a second aunt would call to tell me her side of the story. After listening to both of them, I often concluded that each one was right, and often both of them were wrong—a matter of perspective. Diplomacy in handling the trivial situations was ultimate in my mind. I knew my aunts appreciated that discretion as they vented their grievances to me, and am sure they felt better after talking to me.

Paul and Harry ignored the situations that had manifested. As usual, they remained friendly with Fannie. Her brothers-in-law, as a matter of fact, treated Fannie more like a sister than did her own sisters. It was Paul who, seeing that Fannie could not sell the property on 60th Street, bought the building from her.

Chapter Twelve

*A*lthough my aunt knew the loneliness of single life, she denied ever being lonely. Reading newspapers and books she received as gifts, and which she often brought to our house on visits, filled her time and kept her mind alert. Rarely tuning into television during the day hours, my aunt was not one to watch soap operas. Often the days were too short to finish her planned chores, but by evening, after dinner, she was ready to relax.

During her years of retirement, Fannie became a self- disciplined woman who rarely let anything get in the way of her schedule. The disciplines she followed entered into Fannie's health habits as well as her cleaning and cooking schedule. Following each meal, Fannie disappeared into the bathroom to care for her teeth—a good reason she did not snack between meals. She wanted to keep her teeth intact, although when she stayed overnight with us, I saw a bridge in a glass of water on the bathroom sink, a secret I did not betray.

And each day my aunt brushed her hair one-hundred strokes; a salesman, who sold combs and brushes, had once told my aunt that brushing hair keeps it shining and healthy looking. I think of how strong her right arm had gotten. No

101

one could ever convince her otherwise. Joe, with his usual wit, suggested the exercise was good for her arm. I, of a more somber nature, thought it was good for her spirit. Nonetheless, her hair always held a sheen.

I was quite surprised the day I saw graying strands of hair framing the face of my aunt—the strands the hairdresser had handsomely disguised for so many years. Fannie had heard reports of harmful results from dye chemicals that are applied to the scalp and immediately ceased having her hair colored. Her locks of hair, which she still continued to brush, gradually turned to a glistening white. She was more beautiful to me than she had ever been. Her hair reminded me, in later years, of my grandmother whose facial characteristics of aging were sculpted in the features of my aunt.

The exercise Fannie pursued was the pushing and pulling of the vacuum cleaner, and scrubbing the kitchen floor on her hands and knees. And every day she stretched across the bed to straighten the discolored chenille bedspread. Growing older, my aunt lived under the threat of advisement from a physician—which meant to forego her pride—and lean upon a cane. But Fannie wanted to "stand on her own two feet," fearing eventual confinement in a wheelchair. She knew all of that stretching, pulling and pushing helped to maintain the strength of the rest of her body, including her shoulders and arms. She sensed what was good for her.

But with all of the care she took of herself, Fannie's walk became more unsteady. Within the walls of the three small rooms, Fannie was forced to extend her arms, latching onto the worn furniture, or pressing against a faded wall in order to maintain her balance. Many a time she lost her equilibrium and tripped. It became evident that she could no longer, in her own mind, physically "stand tall." The only course of action, now, was to seek the security of something on which to lean—a cane—clearly a loss of dignity and independence. She had no other choice for bruises blemished her body and bumps swelled on her head too many days in a row. One day, I feared, her falls would lead to a disastrous situation. In her stalwartness, sliced with a fragment of humor, Fannie took satisfaction in the way she fell—that she did not break an arm or a leg, again—or a hip. It was usually her face or head that took the abuse as the weight of her body plunged to the floor.

Meanwhile, no longer did my aunt travel to hear the glorious music at the outdoor concerts she once enjoyed so much. Instead, she stayed close to home working at her chores, reading and listening to the radio, or watching limited television in the evenings.

Realizing she did not leave the house very often in her retirement, neighbors invited Fannie to join them on religious holidays. Knowing she was unable to reciprocate their gracious, repeated offers, Fannie often declined. Once she accepted an invitation, after some insistence, she was happy to be in the company of her hosts and appreciated their consideration. Truly a social person, Fannie enjoyed chatting with her neighbors, catching up on the latest news on the block. Yet, with each invitation, she mulled over in her mind the question, "Do they feel sorry for me because of *my condition*, or do they honestly want my company?" The wry sense of humor and warm sincerity that always set Aunt

Fannie apart in the eyes of strangers concealed her independent nature and overconcern of her physical disability.

Occasionally, Fannie took the bus into the center of town, though not as often, and during daylight hours. Banking at the main office in center city was her prime purpose, even though there were branch banks close by. Doing business with people who recognized her gave Fannie a reassuring feeling. There was, especially, one kind and gentle woman who handled Fannie's transactions for dozens of years, answering her many questions and taking extra good care of her. The women regarded each other with respect and admiration and Fannie cherished the personal care and attention she received. She felt she was dealing with a friend.

Trips to the hairdresser, while in Center City, kept Fannie longer than she wanted to stay. A minimum of activities expended my aunt's energy, and she was exhausted by the time she arrived home. With her walking becoming more difficult, her lameness more prominent now that she was leaning on a cane, Fannie became unnecessarily self-conscious than she ever had been in the past. She sensed all eyes staring at her. She recognized how different she was from the crowds of men and women bustling past her, intent on getting to their destinations as quickly as they could.

Ironically, Fannie's safety was no more guaranteed in her retirement than it had been while working in the store— as she found out on one of her infrequent trips to the downtown bank. Embedded in her memory was that day she waited for the bus on the same corner where she had waited for the many years when she went to work.

The bus Fannie viewed down the street rolled to a stop at

the corner to pick up its passengers. With the strap of her handbag held in one hand, and the handle of the cane gripped firmly in the other, my aunt alighted the first step of the bus. As she lifted the other leg to gain her footing, she was thrown from behind and landed on the sidewalk. Out of nowhere, a young man had grabbed her purse containing money and checks. Her purse with the money for deposit was gone.

The passengers saw the young fellow run away. Not one person made an attempt to catch him. The driver jumped out of his seat from behind the steering wheel and kindly helped his injured passenger onto the bus. He seated her, then drove to the nearest depot where he called the police. None of the passengers registered a complaint that the timing of their destination had been delayed. Trying to calm her, the people on the bus showed an unusual compassion for the disheveled, diminutive woman. In minutes, a cabulance appeared to carry my shaken aunt to the hospital.

Fraught by another attack, Fannie was examined and sent home. Fortunately, this time she was only slightly injured. Though bruised physically, there was no discernible psychological pain.

But I could not understand how Aunt Fannie remained silent about what had to be a severe blow to her psyche. Her attitude appeared to be passive. No signals of distress, only complacency and acceptance. There were no hints of her innermost thoughts, although I am sure that her unwavering religious belief gave her courage. How unnatural, I thought, for someone to experience so much abuse, both physically and mentally, and not show appreciable emotion. I do know, however, that each time something dreadful happened to my aunt, she was grateful that nothing worse had befallen her. Bodily injuries were not as humiliating, perhaps, as the consciousness of the lame leg she dragged with her every step since childhood.

It wasn't long after this latest disturbance that Fannie no longer traveled downtown by public transportation. And it had been a long time since she had an appointment for general examinations concerning her eyes and her teeth. When my aunt was younger, she had been administered numerous injections to combat hay fever suffered through numerous seasons. She had seen enough doctors at the hospitals during her emergencies and received enough medical examinations in her lifetime.

It was out of fear, an undeniable explanation, that she did not seek routine check-ups, or examinations—fear of having an internal ailment or disorder as did her sister, Gertie—in addition to her physical impairment. She did not want to live on medication for the rest of her life. Of course, too, she thought it an imposition to have to ask a niece or nephew, or one of her sisters to drive her to an appointment. But the necessity of arranging transportation arose whenever a dental problem developed.

Aunt Fannie could have called a taxicab to drive her to doctors' offices. Certainly she had the financial means. Was it a matter of so-called "pinching pennies" or apprehension, based on past experiences, of vulnerability—being alone and helpless with the driver of the cab in control of her destination? The discussion frequently arises amongst the cousins. I tend to ponder this question again and again.

With faith to sustain her, Fannie recovered from the last

attack. It was quite coincidental that around the time of Fannie's healing, a girl's youth organization made inquiry to the Jewish Family Service regarding visits to elderly people living in the neighborhood. The timing was perfect.

And so Sara, one of the group members who lived a few blocks away, came with a few of her friends to meet Aunt Fannie. They came regularly each Saturday. The afternoons spent with the young people cheered my aunt. She eagerly looked forward to the Sabbath. Every week a different combination of girls appeared, but Sara was among them almost each time. When the visits seemed to dwindle, it was Sara who continued to call on the woman she came to revere.

Fannie entertained Sara with stories of life in Russia and of her family's escape. Sara heard how Fannie celebrated various holidays when she was a little girl, and particularly Chanukah. Sara heard the stories I had heard as a boy— how, for instance, Fannie had been given a few meager coins as a child, as is the custom during this December holiday, and the warning her mother issued: "Don't lose them, but if you see someone who needs it more than you, give it to them."

Sara enjoyed listening to the stories of Fannie's youth, stories that carried morals, teachings instilled into my aunt's character at an early age, and practiced for the remainder of her life. Fannie related to her youthful visitor how, when she was young, she wanted to visit a "little friend" nearby in the small Russian village. Granting permission, her mother simultaneously stipulated, "If they are eating and offer you food, don't take it. I know you are hungry, but don't take food from other people. Then they won't have enough to eat."

Fannie watched her Sara grow into adulthood. As Sara matured, Fannie passed along the code of living handed down by my grandmother. Bubba had instructed my aunt, in her self-pity, a maxim Fannie abided by all the days of her life: "Be grateful for one's capacities rather than dwell on one's incapacities." Like my generation, Sara has since passed this maxim on to her children. Was it lessons like these that gave Aunt Fannie compassion, that played a part in the molding of her personality and defined her attitude toward life and people?

When Sara married Fannie was invited to the wedding. She was sad, though, that the marriage meant Sara would move to Lakewood in North Jersey with her husband. The two friends, in spite of the wide difference in age, stayed in touch with each other through greeting cards and telephone calls. As the young woman's family grew, she brought her children to visit though the women did not get much of a chance to chat. Fannie was occupied playing and catering to the children. She kept lollipops and bottles of soda for them when they came to see her. Fannie loved children, and they loved her.

Once Sara reached Fannie's house, it was difficult leaving. Sara usually stopped to see her dear friend whom she learned to call "Aunt Fannie," on the way back to Lakewood after having spent some time with her mother. Since it became more and more difficult to get away on each visit, she soon realized it was more efficient to stop at Fannie's house first. Now that Fannie knew Sara's mother was waiting for her, she hastened her on her way before too many hours passed.

The children grew older and Sara became more involved with their activities. Visits to Fannie became less frequent. Still Sara stayed in touch with her dear elderly friend whom she loved and admired. Fannie missed the young woman, the children, and entertaining her guests.

As if it were in a Great Plan children from an elementary school associated with the nearby synagogue, accompanied by their teacher, started to come to Fannie's house. They brought pictures drawn especially for my aunt, and at Purim the children carried *shalech monas*, baskets of sweets. They spent time with Fannie talking and exchanging stories; Fannie delighted in seeing her new little friends. She became "Aunt Fannie" to them, also, just as she was adopted as an aunt by the many people who had grown fond of her.

My aunt thoroughly enjoyed company. It was only in the recent past that she didn't mind people dropping by on Saturdays, or on special holidays without notice since, these were the days she put her chores aside. As she became more confined to her immediate surroundings my aunt yearned to see people.

My own children, having grown close to their great-aunt were sure to see her on their visits home from college. Aunt Fannie, they would tell me, never changed the script of her stories, and I know that they have the recitals nearly memorized. And in the more recent years when our son married, he often took his new bride to Aunt Fannie's apartment for brief visits.

Fannie was always sure to offer food to her guests, even though she refused to eat between meals. Flavored gelatin mixed with slivers of apple rested on the refrigerator shelf, waiting to be shared. Canned tuna was a staple in the cabinet, always available for a sandwich. Fannie knew that some of her guests, no matter what age, liked the Coca Cola which she had stocked on the floor in the closet. Aunt Fannie was excited when her visitors accepted the food or drink she bestowed upon them. She felt like a queen when she was able to share with others. She couldn't give her company enough to eat, and was perturbed when someone declined. Even the adults who dropped by to see her got no lesser treatment than the children. And each of the adults left with a small box of wine samplers wrapped in chaste-white paper embellished with a red bow, the same package she carried to her hosts when she went to their homes. Buying the wine from the Women's Auxiliary at the synagogue was Fannie's contribution toward their fund-raising activities.

The juices of the red fermented grapes took my aunt back to the days when her mother made the sweetest, most delicious-tasting wine. Aunt Fannie's gift was indicative of her sentiments: "To your sweet life."

Chapter Thirteen

*L*ife was not so sweet in the late 1960's for some members of the family. Millie was divorced in the middle of a pregnancy and moved back to Philadelphia where she gave birth to a third child. As a result of the lengthy bout with diabetes, Rosalie's eyesight started to deteriorate, and her husband Milton had suffered a heart attack at an early age.

My father experienced extreme loneliness without my mother. Although he still kept the store open, it was not the flourishing business as when Mom was alive. Joe was still in New England, and I with my family lived some twenty miles away. Other than close friends he had from the time he moved into the small municipality forty-five years ago, my father was left to manage pretty much by himself. Shortly after I moved, having lived a short distance from my parents, Thomas who was a slim man with nervous traits, complained of not feeling well. Ever since I can remember, he had smoked up to two packs of cigarettes a day. After ailing for a few weeks, Thomas went to see the same practitioner who had taken care of Gertie. The doctor was unable make a diagnosis without further examination, and sent him to the hospital to have the necessary tests performed. When the results became known, it was imperative for Thomas to undergo surgery soon after a malignancy on his kidney was discovered. The organ was removed and, at the time, the prognosis looked favorable even though my father stubbornly continued to smoke.

A slow recuperation followed, and Thomas managed the business every day during the business week until the middle of one summer night when the telephone jangled my wife and me awake. It was the police. Startled, I listened carefully to what the officer was saying to make sure I wasn't dreaming. He informed me that he had found my father wandering around town, unaware that everyone else was sound asleep. The lights in the store were burning brilliantly at two o'clock in the morning. just as if he were open for business at that hour.

A few days later I brought my father to our house, and made arrangements for him to enter a nearby nursing home. Within a year from his initial surgery, the cancer had spread. It was a short stay at the nursing home, for he entered the hospital and turned critically ill. It was there that he died.

Aunt Fannie lost the two people she respected the most—first a sister, and now a brother-in-law—both of whom had encouraged her in the business, contributing to her independence. The emptiness was intense. Fannie grieved with my brother and me, for both my mother and father were dead.

My aunt's empathy prompted her to telephone me on Sundays at approximately 10 o'clock in the morning—the same day and hour I used to talk to my parents. Committed to the continuity of family ties, Aunt Fannie made every effort to maintain them, at least with my brother and me.

But my aunt's hopes for a peaceful relationship with her sisters dissolved as quickly as sugar disintegrates in hot water. Differences mounted through each of their sarcastic and sensitive natures. There was no one to reconcile disagreements amongst the sisters. I was available only to listen to them.

Unquestionably, Fannie was envious of both Minnie and Bella. Minnie and Harry had made plans to sail around the world in celebration of their fiftieth wedding anniversary. Fannie was resentful that her sisters had physical and financial capabilities she did not—and husbands to accompany them wherever they wanted to go.

Sparks occasionally flew from the tongues of both sisters. There was no real way to resolve the confrontations. A cooling-off period cleared the air for short periods of time, although Minnie continued to be concerned about her older sister's health.

My aunts put me in the middle of their bickering, for within a week's time, I had heard both sides of a story. With reservation I listened to each of them in an effort to be discerning, as my mother would have done. I attempted to keep most of my thoughts to myself, for I didn't want to play one against the other. I was aware of the virtues claimed by each of them, as well as their frailties. I respected them singly for their redeeming qualities and loved them equally.

The repeated entreaty of my grandmother to Minnie and Bella to look after Fannie was all but forgotten. Fannie prayed for peace between her sisters and herself. With a shrug of her narrow shoulders, she questioned, "What can I do about it?" In answer to her own question, she followed it with "That's the way they are."

The hurt was deep-rooted, and the elderly, spiritual woman accepted it on their terms.

Minnie and Bella sold their homes in West Philadelphia and moved to fashionable high-rise complexes. Minnie was situated close to the center of the city, but Bella stayed in the same general area in which she lived.

Rosalie had long moved away from the area, she and her husband having bought a house in another suburb of Philadelphia. A few years later they made a decision to settle across the river in New Jersey. Millie, who remarried, bought a property within a short distance from Aunt Fannie's house. The family was dispersed, yet close enough to see each other on holidays and at celebrations.

One by one, the neighbors on Aunt Fannie's block put their houses up for sale. All, that is, except for Jake across the street. Within a few years time, he and my aunt were the only old-time residents on the street. Fannie would not consider moving. Where would she go? She wished to stay in her small apartment for the rest of her life, secure in her memories, and possessing all the comforts she ever needed.

Fannie was virtually alone. The telephone kept her close to old and dear friends, and as new neighbors moved into the empty houses on Malvern Avenue my aunt made new friends. But the people with whom Fannie sensed the closest ties, who understood her trusting and naive ways, had abandoned her through circumstances over which no human has control. Fate was in command, for first Bubba had died, followed by Gertie and Thomas.

Then, in 1969, Fannie's girlfriend Sonia passed away. While Fannie was busy doing her usual chores one day, the telephone rang. She picked up the receiver, and heard a familiar voice—a voice filled with grief and tears. It was Ben, Sonia's son. Through his sobs she wondered if she heard him correctly. "Aunt Fannie, my mother was hit by a car on the way to work. She died instantly."

"What did you say?" she asked, unwilling to believe the mournful news. When he repeated the statement, a shriek vibrated through the wires followed by sheer silence. Gasps interrupted Ben's talking. Hysterical, Fannie hung up, unable to speak a word.

Later in the day, Ben, concerned about his mother's close friend, called Fannie to see if she was all right. Fannie was perturbed, enraged, confused, all at the same time. There was no warning, no signal, no illness that preceded Sonia's death. Fannie was overwrought, so much so that she was unable to attend the funeral.

The friendship with Fannie generated a unique relationship between Ben and the woman he came to adopt as an aunt. Ben became devoted to Aunt Fannie after Sonia died. In his thirties, he had married and moved to Levittown, Pennsylvania.

Phyllis and Ben invited Aunt Fannie into their home on holidays and many other occasions. Fannie persistently refused to stay overnight. Aside from preferring the comfort of her own bed, she thought she was imposing upon other people if she accepted their invitations. The stubbornness of her personality was as transparent as her compassion.

It amazed Fannie's new family to listen to this "woman of valor," a fitting description which Phyllis gave the praiseworthy woman. Phyllis and Ben lauded their inherited aunt for the manner in which she surmounted countless obstacles in her life, the fact that she was lame, yet, "she did not allow much to get in her way." Endeavors of self-sufficiency—and plain stubbornness—deterred Fannie from obvious limitations that a person of lesser character may have self-imposed.

There was a time when Ben did talk Fannie into staying overnight. She loved the attention he and his family lavished on her, and Fannie showed a genuine interest in Ben's and Phyllis's two boys. Sean and Joshua appreciated the intensity of Fannie's convictions, and told their friends that the *aunt* "is unrelated, but related to us."

Joshua extended an invitation to Aunt Fannie to see "Oklahoma," a musical which his high school had sponsored. Joshua had a part in the play and was anxious for Fannie to see him in his role. Thrilled at being invited to the performance, Fannie could not believe young people that age were capable of such fine acting. She considered it a very professional performance—"like real actors on the stage." For Joshua there could be no greater compliment.

Sean and Joshua heard the same stories Aunt Fannie had told my cousins and me, and my children, over and over again. The boys savored the details which enlightened them to the history of her younger life, and to an epoch in the history of former Russia. The brothers had difficulty, though, distinguishing whether the circumstances in the stories occurred at different times, or if Fannie was reciting the same story many times over. I think, after several repetitions, they figured out which of the two options was accurate.

On yet another of Fannie's visits, Russian acquaintances were invited to join Phyllis and Ben for an afternoon. Fannie couldn't have been happier. Although she had not spoken her native tongue for a very long time, she remembered more Russian than she thought she had. Words that had a special meaning remained with my aunt for many decades. Fannie was excited hearing the language spoken fluently once again, and tried to interpret words that the new Russian immigrants were saying. The kinship bonded by the language which was foreign to her hosts, was interspersed with a bit of Yiddish dialect, the homogenous tongue Fannie spoke when her mother was still alive.

Even now I can hear her speaking the language, stopping to ask, "Do you understand Yiddish?" She spoke expressions in Yiddish to better express a point.

My unassuming aunt played an influential role in the lives of the two boys during the time Ben and his wife Phyllis were raising their children. She had earned the respect of Sean and Joshua just as she earned the respect of the young neighborhood boys who played ball in the back alley under the street light in the late summer evenings.

Fannie had a way with young people. I think it was the kind, sincere way she treated them. At times the boys were noisier than usual. They seemingly started their games when my aunt was ready to retire for the evening. Fannie would then raise the bedroom window to get their attention and tell them she was an old lady who needed her rest. She politely suggested they move elsewhere. Without a word directed toward her, the children left.

It was not long before Fannie earned the admiration of not only the boys who played near her house, but many of the new neighbors who had moved into nearby houses. They got to know her and her habits well.

A black woman who lived on the other side of the street took it upon herself to telephone "Miss Fannie" every day. She checked to be sure my aunt was all right, and asked Fannie if she needed anything. The woman knew my aunt's legs were growing more wobbly, and her falls increasing— interferences my aunt refused to accept. The side of her body which had sustained the full weight of her walking for all of these years was wearing down. She trudged along, her figure swaying often. In objection to giving in and sitting for most of the day, she was well aware that keeping busy on her feet was the mainstay of her well-being. Thus she plodded on with her daily tasks, just as she had in the past, though at a much slower pace.

And so it was not unusual that on the scheduled day of the week, Fannie descended the basement steps to do her laundry. I was afraid that one day she might topple down the darkly-lit stairs. I asked her why she did not launder the few pieces in the kitchen sink.

"Nobody washes clothes in the kitchen sink," she insisted. "The sink is to wash dishes in," intimating that personal garments were to be laundered where her mother had always done the "wash" in the basement.

I admit it was more convenient to hang dripping articles on the clothesline in the basement to dry. Why should she suddenly change an ingrained habit? She had already changed so many others! As it were, each week she made her way to the dark, dank basement. My aunt knew the telephone would ring once she started her work, and didn't want to risk hurrying up the stairs only to have someone hang up when she picked up the phone. After carrying the clothes downstairs, she would make her way up the steps again to get the black telephone with its elongated cord. Then she laid the heavy instrument on one of the lower steps, a convenient place should someone call, where she could sit on the basement step to talk. After hanging the clothes on the line, Fannie, telephone in hand, lumbered back upstairs. Only that morning she forgot to pull the wire all the way in front of her. Half way up the steps, her mind ahead of her feet, Fannie plummeted to the cement floor.

For hours she lay on the cool, damp surface. The neighbor who had called daily received no answer that day. The woman panicked. She called Paul who rushed over immediately. Having no key to enter the house, Paul had to break the porch window which faced the street. Then he carefully climbed in and noticed the door to the basement ajar. Running toward it Paul bounded down the steps where he saw his sister-in-law lying motionless on the basement floor.

An ambulance came to take Fannie to the hospital. Her arm started to swell, and the X-rays indicated some broken bones. My aunt was forced to stay at the hospital until the broken bones were set and a new cast dressed her arm. Her body was badly bruised, but again she was thankful it was not a worse disaster.

Minnie telephoned me in near hysteria. She had just found out about Fannie's latest accident. "What are we going to do?" she cried to me. "She can't stay by herself."

I was not the least bit surprised at Minnie's involvement with Fannie. She wanted to get to the hospital as soon as possible, but Harry was nowhere to be reached. So she asked me to drive from my house in New Jersey to Philadelphia, pick her up at the apartment and take her to see Fannie. I left my house at once while Minnie waited for me in the lobby of her apartment house so we would not lose any time.

With a cast up to her elbow again, Fannie was unable to care for herself after she arrived home. The instability of her legs, and the cast on her arm, were new reminders for my accident-prone aunt to exercise extra caution in the apartment.

Minnie was disgruntled over the numerous accidents and bad luck that had befallen her sister, and the existing dependency upon Harry and herself. Nonetheless, if a little ruefully, she upheld her responsibility toward her crippled sister. Minnie ordered prepared hot meals to be delivered while Fannie was recovering from the latest trauma. A few days of eating someone else's cooking was not to Fannie's liking, and she called a halt to the deliveries. Once more it fell upon Bella and Minnie to prepare Fannie's meals and take them to her.

Bella and Minnie persevered in their attempt to make life easier for Fannie. They called the Jewish Family Service to hire a woman a few hours a day to help wash and dress Fannie, prepare a few meals and, perhaps, do light cleaning. Without notice Fannie dismissed the aide after she had worked for a few days. My aunt was annoyed at having unfamiliar people hover around her. But her sisters were

120

enraged with Fannie's control of matters. They made an effort to take care of their sister, and at the same time make things easier for themselves. All the while, Fannie resisted. Minnie's indignation grew worse. She was, after all, doing what she could for Fannie's comfort and convenience. It appeared her sister did not appreciate that, when in truth, Fannie resented someone taking over and making decisions for her. She failed to realize that her siblings were trying to make their own lives less complicated, as well.

Fannie sat home and read while her arm healed. Reading newspapers proved slow and laborious while Fannie absorbed every word. Interest in world news kept her updated, but her eyes were not as good as they had once been, and her mind did not concentrate as it once had. My aunt read passages from her prayer book studying them carefully, over and over, hypnotizing herself to sleep.

During the recuperative period, Fannie had many moments to reflect upon the past.

Fannie was confined to her surroundings. There were no more bus trips downtown to take care of her financial business. Most of the banking by now was done by mail. Once in a while Millie stopped by the house to cash checks for her, and occasionally my aunt requested me to take her into Center City to the hairdresser.

Ben and Phyllis once remarked to me how cloistered Fannie's life had become, and they realized how unaware she was of latest technological developments, such as computers and home video films. When she heard an answering machine for the first time upon calling Ben's house, she was distraught. Ben did not answer the telephone personally; it was only the recording of his voice she heard. She thought he had died. She left a message, however, screaming, "Where are you? Why is this thing on? What is this?" The new computer age confounded her.

I saw my aunt growing older, more bent as she steadied herself in walking. Few wrinkles marked her face, though her white hair glistened with the years. I recognized changes taking place while her memory slipped, and sleep crept in more frequently during daylight hours.

Fannie accepted her lot for there was no recourse.

Chapter Fourteen

*T*he telephone rang in Fannie's house. It was the real estate agent. As in the past the realtor had attempted to rent the upstairs rooms, but more often the arrangements did not suit either Fannie, or the prospective tenant. This time my aunt was told over the telephone that a young black woman, interested in looking at the vacant apartment, was in his office.

Fannie responded, "Bring her. If she likes what she sees, maybe I'll rent it to her." Soon after the inspection, the young woman, Dolores, moved in with her few belongings. The agent collected the moderate rental fee which he in turn sent to Aunt Fannie.

The apartment was so quiet that, at times, Aunt Fannie forgot there was anyone living in the rooms above her. Fannie never heard the radio or the television. Each day her new tenant went to work, and each evening she returned. My aunt was happy with the agreement. She knew that, finally, she housed a pleasant, considerate person in her upstairs apartment, and a person with whom she could exchange a few words.

Dolores had become more than a renter. She became Fannie's friend who carried out small favors for her landlady.

She watched the apartment and collected the mail the infrequent times Fannie came to stay a night or two at our house. In general, the young woman kept a watch over my aunt.

At times Jeannine and I were able to convince Fannie, who was becoming a recluse, to leave the house and spend a few days with us. She protested that the time away from her house interfered with her rigid schedule, but I was persistent and usually won out. She needed a change of scenery and some lively conversation even though she said she was content to be at home. Fannie continued to go to Ben and Phyllis' house for birthdays and holidays, but only for the day, and those visits were growing less frequent.

Aunt Fannie would pack her suitcase, and wait anxiously for me to pull up in front of her house. She worried if I was a little late, and called my wife to see where I was. As we drove across the bridge to New Jersey, Aunt Fannie remarked gratefully, "Such a long distance—and you came to get me."

Once in the house, Aunt Fannie removed her coat and greeted my wife. Each time she came, before I carried her suitcase upstairs to the guest room my aunt, without fail, opened her suitcase and pulled a package from it, a box wrapped in spotless white paper captioned with a red bow. Presenting us with samplers of wine, the gift had become my aunt's trademark.

Our collection of wine grew with each visit no matter if we went to Fannie's house, or she came to visit us. The bottles accumulated since my wife and I drink little, and that only at celebrations. But we could not refuse the gift given sincerely from the heart.

Out of the suitcase also appeared a stained apron which Fannie hung on the back of a kitchen chair, ready to help with the cooking and the cleaning up after dinner. Even though Jeannine usually dislikes anyone standing in the small area near the sink where she prepares meals, she managed to find a job to keep my aunt occupied. Late in the afternoon, Fannie could be found leaning over the sink and resting on one leg, slowly peeling carrots, or potatoes, or cutting ends off the string beans. A menial task, perhaps, but enough work to relieve Aunt Fannie's impression that it was an imposition to have her with us.

When she expects guests, my wife sets out a clean washcloth and towel on the yellow sink in the upstairs bathroom. Yet Aunt Fannie insisted on bringing her own linens. In consideration for her hosts, it is her way to reduce our work, even though we have a washer and dryer, and she must send her linens to a commercial laundry to be washed and pressed. Understanding her well-meaning deeds, we let the situation rest.

Since the rabbi from the synagogue which Fannie attended had retired, Jeannine and I extended an invitation for her to be with us during the High Holidays. This gave my aunt the opportunity to attend services and not have to worry how she was going to get to her neighborhood synagogue. My wife and I were proud to have Aunt Fannie sit between us while we prayed, and she was overjoyed at not having to be alone on this sacred holiday. She was with a part of her family.

Our friends and relatives whom we saw at services got

to know her, recognizing her from year to year. They looked forward to greeting her during the holidays and accepted Fannie cordially.

Following one of the evening services, before the days Aunt Fannie depended on a cane, Jeannine, my aunt and I were walking down the freshly-waxed hall to the front of the building. Before any one of us knew it, the heel of Fannie's lame foot slipped from under her. The back of her head hit the floor. As this was the first time my wife and I witnessed such a tumble, we were more frightened than she. Aunt Fannie got up slowly and said she was all right. She reassured us that she knows how to fall, and accepted the impact without complaint.

To our distress, we were there to witness another fall. It occurred during a subsequent visit as we were getting into the car. This time Aunt Fannie was fortunate to land on the soft grass at the curb. It very well could have been the concrete pavement! Jeannine and I knew of the bumps on her head. We had seen the black and blue bruises on her arms confirming that falls now were a pattern, a sequence acknowledged by my aunt in the course of her failing balance.

This was the reason my aunt finally relented to the use of a cane. She needed something to lean on, to support the shrinking weight of her body. Too proud to graduate to a walker, which was almost a necessary accompaniment at this stage, Fannie dreaded the thought of a succeeding phase. Inevitably it would be a wheelchair. This was something she would never allow to happen. "I would rather die first." She spoke unequivocally.

The drying scabs she often showed us on her scalp—

where blood oozed through her white wavy hair—were proof enough of the abuse her head took from the falls onto the thinning carpets and hard floors in her apartment.

It was then I knew a change was imperative in order that my aunt not be alone for most of the day. Time was growing closer to an adjustment of other sorts, perhaps the hiring of a housekeeper to allay my fears, at least for now. Self-esteem, or the same innate stubbornness previously displayed, deterred my aunt from even thinking about a senior-citizen retirement home even though I proceeded to dwell on the idea.

I know my aunt heard the concern in my voice, anxieties that echoed those of her nieces and other nephew. She always listened thoughtfully, though it seemed I spoke in vain. Despite all the reasons I could think of, Aunt Fannie fought the idea of abandoning the security of her home. She opposed it with all the stubborn powers of her independence.

To Fannie such a thought conjured up visions of being placed in an "old age home" with the repugnance it signified—forgotten by friends and family—and left to die. No wonder she wanted to stay in her own home until she could no longer stand on her feet. "What will be, will be," she repeated often. I understood what she was telling me. It did not take much to interpret the meaning of her words "God will watch over me." Someone was watching over Aunt Fannie, for she had passed her eightieth year of life.

It was somewhere during this decade in her life that, in the middle of one night when Aunt Fannie slept at our house, Jeannine heard a dull thump. Awakened by the sound, my wife peered between the partially-open door of our bedroom hoping that she was dreaming. But her opened eyes did not betray what was visible in the dim glow of the nightlight. While I lay beside her in a quiet, deep sleep, Jeannine caught a glimpse of a frightening sight. Aunt Fannie was crawling toward the bathroom on her hands and knees! My wife didn't know what to do. Emotionally distressed, she lay there physically frozen, listening for Fannie to return safely to her room. Minutes felt like hours until my wife was able to fall back to sleep. It is a memory that will never vanish from her mind.

The next morning Jeannine said nothing. But during the conversation at breakfast Aunt Fannie told us what she had done during the night—and why. Her explanation took us by surprise, yet sounded logical, even overly thoughtful of my wife and me.

Aunt Fannie did not want to chance falling which would, in turn, awaken us. Instead of risk landing noisily on the floor, she got down on her hands and knees to get to the bathroom. The next night at her insistence, she slept downstairs on the sofa close to the powder room. Thinking of her comfort, we let her have her way. All three of us spent a restless night.

Fannie and I had many lively conversations, and some disagreements, while she stayed with us. She was an interesting person to talk to, and our conversations ranged from education to history to politics. I updated my aunt with events while she listened enthusiastically and questioned earnestly. Over the years, Fannie had formulated many opinions about current happenings—often biased from her European background. Our conversations always sparkled with predilections.

We had our heated discussions and differences of opinions, each one challenging the other. I attempted, with much difficulty, to open her mind from her narrow viewpoints in regard to world situations. When the time came for her to leave she was both sad and happy—sad that she had to leave us, but happy to return to her predictable schedule with the same satisfaction that routine brings most human beings.

When I drove Aunt Fannie back home, in her later years, she often asked me to stop at the store to buy a loaf of bread. I was happy to accommodate her wish knowing that bread is one of the staples in her diet. It wasn't until I had done this favor repeatedly that, to my astonishment, I discovered the food was not for her. My aunt was feeding the bread to the birds which arrived chattering on the front porch each morning. Aunt Fannie, a sensitive soul into late age, opened the storm door and tossed the morsels of bread as far as the force of her arm could carry them. She fed the birds all year round, which included the extremely cold days of the winters.

There was a joy in having her feathered friends depend on her—to look forward to her generosity, just as she depended upon them to sing their cheerful songs to her. Each day Fannie fed them she, in her heart, knew she was doing a good deed. The small birds seemed to sense that when the front door opened they would have a feast. My aunt was oblivious to the dried white droppings which the rains rarely reached to wash away. That was secondary to the kindness she offered the creatures of nature. If Fannie forgot to put the bread out for them, as sometimes she did, the birds bumped up against the glass storm door to remind the elderly woman it was time for them to eat.

"Oh, I forgot to feed the birds," she would say as quickly as she managed to tear the tiny pieces of bread.

Sitting on the folding chair in the living room, a plate on her lap, Aunt Fannie's arthritic fingers pulled the soft, white bread apart. As she prepared the bread for the winged creatures, she recurrently reflected upon herself as a little girl when her mother called her by an endearing Yiddish name, *Fagiele*—little bird.

My aunt was sensitive to the needs of living creatures. She felt their helplessness and their hunger. While she and I waited for Jeannine to prepare breakfast one morning at our house, our cat was underfoot meowing for her first meal of the day. It was then that Aunt Fannie expounded from Deuteronomy, a section from the Old Testament: "...to show compassion for animals by feeding them before we feed ourselves."

Fannie believed that all life is in God's hands, and that humans should care for animals as well as care for each other.

Chapter Fifteen

*J*ust as the birds looked forward to the bread Fannie fed them each day, Fannie looked forward to seeing her sister, Bella. In more recent years Bella, the short slim sister who, for most of her life, wore her titian hair pulled up in a bun, had been the liaison between Minnie and Fannie. And by now, she and Fannie were able to view things in the same perspective. They had become more compatible. I think that with age each of them had mellowed.

Now that Bella retired from the business, and Nora was living away from home, Bella had more time and was willing to make life easier for her sister, Fannie. The laundry which was already being handled by a service freed Bella from a previous obligation. But Bella, who knew Fannie had no one other than herself to depend on for food shopping continued, for all of these years, to buy the groceries for her sister. Each week Fannie had a list ready, and each week Bella returned from the store with her arms full of groceries. The bags contained much the same items week after week: canned tuna, frozen vegetables, flavored gelatin, apples, eggs and cookies or crackers. My aunt's favorite sesame seed cookies, to which she treated herself, went down well with the tea she drank at lunch and dinner.

Fannie eagerly sought the chance to see Bella and speak to her. She always said that looking directly at a person, catching the expression on his or her face gave her a different perspective from hearing only the tone of a voice over the telephone. Bella, it seemed though, was often in a hurry and unable to spend much time with her sister.

What a shock it was when, suddenly, Bella became ill in the fall of 1982. Suffering sharp pains in her chest and down her arm, she was rushed to the hospital by ambulance. It was a critical situation from the first. One night Bella took a turn for the worse; she died soon thereafter. Now it was Paul who was without a wife, and Nora who was without a mother.

Fannie lamented the loss of a third sister. This time she grieved, also, for a brother-in -law whose wife had pampered him throughout their marriage, and who helped him in the business. Bella had, after all, undertaken the responsibilities a woman in the 1940's assumed upon reciting the marriage vows—caring completely for the welfare of her husband, child and household. For Nora, Fannie felt only pity.

There was no Bella to talk to, the acquiescent sibling whose face always appeared drained from the demands of a husband and daughter. Feeling very much alone, Fannie agonized over her younger sister and all that Bella had done for her. A deep expression of appreciation was left mostly unsaid. The regret lay deep in Fannie's conscience. She was left with only a mixture of memories.

Following the death of Bella, it was not remarkable to find Fannie doleful for the long period she grieved. As well as being doleful, my aunt was also perplexed. After the funeral when the mourners gathered at Bella's house I heard Aunt Fannie ask the rabbi, "Why do my sisters who have husbands and children die before me? I have no one to live for. They have their families who need them."

Too often, Aunt Fannie pondered illness and dying those days, and probed God's reasoning in the sequence of her sisters' deaths. With reserve, as a clergy who no doubt has answered similar questions, the rabbi unhesitantly responded, "Because it is not your turn." For the moment the reply appeased Fannie. She accepted the philosophy of the ordained man as if it were an answer from the Almighty himself.

From the moment Bella died, Fannie was left to stand up to Minnie on her own. She no longer expected her one surviving sister to show the same concern for her as she had many years ago. The two sisters had grown apart. From now on Fannie would have to fend for herself.

Thank goodness for the chores which kept Aunt Fannie busy in the small apartment. Still, her days were filled with tears, and her mind filled with questions. Thoughts of her dead sisters could not escape her. Though the activities kept her physically moving, she was lonelier than she had ever been. The tempo of her movements languished, and the days stretched despite visits from neighbors and friends who occasionally stopped by, or the people whose voices she heard over the telephone. Fannie rarely spoke to Minnie anymore. Her heart ached for her dead sisters, even though her two brothers-in-law called and visited on a regular schedule.

Through stories echoed at opportune times, Fannie embraced the memories of Gertie and Bella. The repeated stories were segments of her mental diary which she added to all of the other recorded memories—the memorized history of her family. Amazing as it was, she had incurred memory loss for details of the present, yet events which occurred many years ago were mentally embedded, never changing. But that is part of human science, I understand.

And she became increasingly perturbed about her memory not being as good as it once had been. Aunt Fannie's generosity never meant to cease, even though she became more frugal as she grew older. Her gracious gifts slackened only because she had neglected to refer to the calendar on which the dates were recorded. A celebrant most often received an apology from Aunt Fannie by telephone.

Ben handled the issue delicately when Fannie called to tell him she forgot it was his birthday. When she wished him a personal birthday greeting and offered an apology, he, being of a gentle nature, casually replied that his birthday had not yet arrived, although the date had well passed.

All of us continued to assure my aunt, and it was necessary to reassure her, that people who have been granted the same amount of years as she suffer memory lapse—that the episode is not unusual, just annoying. I tried to impress upon her, with little success, that people who are much younger than she have trouble remembering important things. I also told her there were many things I forgot, and that I had to jot down notes in order to remember certain details. Still, it was difficult to convince my aunt that this happens to many other people.

Aunt Fannie's memory flourished in other areas, though. In many ways, my aunt was a "wise old bird," as she mentally reviewed her finances frequently for the sake of self-assurance. Although she always retained a written record of the transactions, my aunt remembered her schedule of financial accounts without looking in her books. But the fear that her physical needs would become subject under someone else's management became a monumental one. And she wanted to be capable of paying for those needs with help from no one.

Prudence was a part of Fannie's character that stemmed from her background. But the frugality my aunt practiced often paralleled the illogical. It was this discipline, in fact, that had caused the latest accident, and the mystery of how she injured herself unfolded within a few days after she entered the hospital.

Each morning my aunt poured water into a pot which she placed on a burner on the stove. After the water boiled, she then carried it from the kitchen into the bathroom to wash herself. Fannie's rationale was that turning the faucet on until the water ran hot wasted both water and the gas which heated the water. With one hand holding the pot of water, and the other holding onto the wall, Fannie either faltered in her walking or became light-headed, which caused her to lose her balance and fall. In this instance frugality superseded logic. Aunt Fannie did not consider the cost of the gas emitted from the stove burner to bring the temperature of the liquid to a boiling point. This was one of her foolish means of saving money which brought her pain and anxiety—and another hospital stay. It was one more reason for me to worry about her.

My aunt's means of saving money sometimes sadly, sometimes comically, was also a means of procrastinating.

In the long run a repair had to be done, or a replacement made, despite her economical intentions.

For example, Aunt Fannie thought herself clever when she tied a rag dipped in salt water around a leaking water pipe in the basement. The water seeped through, nonetheless, perhaps slower than it otherwise would have, and eventually my aunt had to call a plumber to replace the pipe.

Indeed, there were many repairs in the house that warranted attention and replacements that had to be made, a fact I was only too aware of and mentioned frequently to her. The refrigerator remained faithful even though it had minor repairs through all of those years. Aunt Fannie really could have used a new one.

"What do I need it for?" was her customary question which embraced its own answer.

To Fannie saving meant denial. She was thrifty so she could give monetary gifts to others—and it gave her great satisfaction to write a check for someone else's pleasure. My aunt always thought that another person, or a charitable institution, could put the money to better use than she. It was the way she had been brought up. The generosity of her character glimmered through her charitable ways. She sought nothing in return. She gave out of the goodness of her heart, and for the spirit of her soul.

Material needs were few for Aunt Fannie. She wore her old clothes, the same few dresses she had owned—I can't begin to remember for how many years—with costume jewelry to complement each dress. The clothes were faded, and very much out of style. She mended her underwear as best she could, salvaging it to make it last longer. Her attire also included mended hosiery which now hung baggy around her thin legs. The only purchase my aunt ever requested was a special brand of support hosiery to wear when she got dressed to go somewhere special.

The unmatched dishes in the cabinets were chipped— the same dishes my aunt had been using since she retired from the store, and probably even before that. The single replacement she ever wanted was a cup and saucer similar to the one she had before. When I brought her some mugs, instead, Aunt Fannie was offended. "You only drink tea from a cup and saucer," she admonished.

I guess change is difficult in old age. I know that shifting habits of cleaning house did not come easily. Rather than using the vacuum cleaner, whereby Fannie might lose her balance she, instead, swept the carpet on her hands and knees with a whisk broom, getting the dirt up with weakened hands and arms. But my aunt knelt with humility!

Scrubbing the narrow kitchen floor on her knees, too, was no small feat for my aunt. Every Friday the floor had to be clean for the Sabbath. And she wanted to wash it herself. Mentally and physically, the exercise did her good. Moving and wriggling eased the stiffness in her unreliable body, and Fannie made an everlasting effort to keep moving on her own will until her final day on earth.

I wondered how much dust and dirt she missed with the degenerating eyesight she suffered. The lenses of her glasses were not changed in recent years, and cataracts may have contributed to the condition. There was no way of knowing, and Aunt Fannie never wanted to find out with a visit to an eye doctor. She was upset, though, that she could no longer see to read as well as she once did, try though she might, since reading was one of her favorite pastimes. Deteriorating eyesight that comes with aging was another fact of life to Aunt Fannie.

Otherwise, Aunt Fannie acceded to whatever else came her way. She also refused to submit to medication. She made no attempt to prolong her life and chose to let nature take its course. She suffered through falls and broken bones and muggings. Remembering her younger sister, Rose, who died in Russia, Aunt Fannie had outlived three sisters. "What good are doctors going to do me now?" she would ask, paralleling her other standard question, "What do I need it for?

Joe was content that Aunt Fannie was eating a well-balanced diet. He strongly believed that the nourishing food added to her well-being. All the same, he recommended she take a multiple vitamin each day. Trusting her nephew's advice, frequently mixed with a spoonful of dry humor, she added a vitamin as part of her morning routine.

Good food and a balanced diet were always important to Aunt Fannie. It was one aspect of her life my aunt did not economize on. But now, since Bella's death, Fannie had to find someone to do the marketing for her. Reluctant to ask Minnie to pick up the few items, she needed to think of someone she could rely on to buy her few parcels of staples. She knew she couldn't count on her tenant, Dolores. She went to work everyday and her weekends were filled with chores of her own. Besides, Dolores didn't own a car to conveniently bring home many bags at one time.

Suddenly Jake entered her mind. Jake was retired and

lived alone just across the street. He drove, and had to go to the store for himself, she thought. One day Fannie summoned the courage to telephone him and ask if he would mind doing the favor of buying her groceries each week. Jake was happy to comply. He sounded glad to help his neighbor out. Fannie always had her short list and money ready for him on the appointed day.

It was a convenient arrangement for which Jake received remuneration for gasoline. The compensation, however, turned out to be more than a barter for Jake. He had gained a girlfriend. My aunt had become friendly with a woman who lived near Malvern Avenue. Frances periodically called my aunt on the telephone to inquire about her health and find out if there was any news from the neighbors, or relatives. A few weeks went by until Frances realized someone was marketing for Fannie. When she found out she asked, "Who is that man that does the shopping for you?"

"It's Jake, the man across the street," Fannie answered.

Frances asked more questions about Jake. Following a few more phone calls, she urged my aunt, "Give him my telephone number."

Fannie could not understand why her friend requested such a thing. "Why would you want me to give him your telephone number? He doesn't even know you," Fannie insisted. After some coaxing, she eventually relented. The next time Fannie spoke to Jake she told him about Frances and gave him her telephone number. As a result, a friendship blossomed between the two strangers. Unwittingly Fannie had become a matchmaker.

PART V

THE LONE SURVIVOR

Chapter Sixteen

*I*n the years following Bella's passing, the confrontations between my two remaining aunts progressed as before, paradoxically, in spite of the fact they rarely spoke to each other. In the few and far times between their conversations, there was always an issue they could not agree on, no matter what. Thus, it was my telephone that rang after one sister had hung up after talking to the other sister. Invariably, one or the other called me at home. They asked volatile questions of me such as, "Why did she do this or that?" or "What made her say such a thing?" engaging me more as a referee between the two of them. Trifling matters turned into overwhelming ones as I maintained my position as diplomat. I can't tell you how unpleasant it was for me to view a situation of this scope between the two surviving sisters.

An overheated argument between them resulted in the absence of Fannie at the marriage of her own grandniece—Rosalie's daughter. Thus, Minnie found herself in the middle of the controversy involving Fannie and Rosalie. An overflow of accusations filled the air, and the air became electrified with emotion.

Of course there had been times before this particular

episode that disagreements between aunt and niece had arisen. Rosalie often found reason to disassociate herself over insignificant matters from the woman she had once thought of as a beloved aunt. This time the embroilment reached its height. Rosalie, embittered over her progressive blindness—incensed that she had such a horrendous thing happening to her—was unable to cope with a particular issue Fannie signalized. It was years before Rosalie spoke to Aunt Fannie. By the time she did, Rosalie had become legally blind.

Minnie's younger daughter, Millie, did not breed hostility as deeply. Perhaps it was because she had been away from the area for so long, and when she did move back, she did not want to get caught up in the web. Her days were filled raising her three children, and two step-children from a second marriage. In the meantime she had started a business.

I think, subconsciously, Minnie resented Fannie from the time she was left behind in Russia with the cousins until money was sent for her to catch up with the group. Fannie had never been one of Minnie's favorite sisters, and after the wedding there was a long silence between them. When one of the sisters had the slightest familial impulse to reveal concern for the other, and dial her number on the telephone, the conversation was chilly and calculating.

The situation between my two aunts did not help the ulcer Minnie suffered within the more recent years. Some days she felt better than others, though she followed a prescribed diet and took her medication. I found out that she had further complaints and was not feeling up to her usual self. One of the appointments with her doctor led to medical tests—tests that indicated a diagnosis of cancer.

Minnie was in and out of the hospital after the report had been made. A few months later came ultimate prognosis. The cancer had metastasized. Nothing further could be done for her. Suffering with increasing pain, Minnie was sent home to live out the rest of her life as best she could.

During her final months, Minnie did not want to see or hear from Fannie. She had no use for her. Minnie did not want the external pain aggravated by a meeting with Fannie, nor did she want overt sympathy from her older sister.

Then in the spring of 1984, Minnie's pain was simply unbearable. Her condition had worsened. She entered the hospital, and all of us knew she would never come home again. We knew the end was near. Upon hearing the gravity of her sister's prognosis, Aunt Fannie called to tell me she wished to see Minnie. She asked for my opinion in deciding what she should do.

"Let me think about it," was the best answer I could give her at the time. I made an effort to delay such a consequential decision, for my aunt had placed me in a weighty position; the decision had to be founded on the deepest sentiments of both aunts. In whose favor was I going to abide, and how was I going to justify my verdict?

That dilemma became a topic of discussion in our household for a few days. After much debate, Jeannine and I concluded that, in order to absolve any guilt she might later feel, Fannie should pay a final visit to her sister even though Minnie's daughter and son-in-law strongly opposed the idea.

After I told Aunt Fannie the conclusion I reached, she

143

called Harry on the telephone. In a quiet tone she said to him, "I would like to see Minnie. Can you take me to the hospital the next time you go?" There was no pressure on Fannie's part, and Harry unconditionally agreed to take her.

On the day of Fannie's visit, Minnie had been alert and talkative. Fannie limped into the hospital room unannounced ahead of Harry. Suddenly Minnie looked up and saw her sister. Rage burned inside her cancer-riddled body—to think that it was her own husband who brought the sister she disliked so much—and against her wishes, no less. Somehow Minnie summoned the strength to scream, "Why did you come? To see me die?"

Was it a coincidence that my wife and I were there to witness the scene, just ready to leave?

Numbed by the outburst, Fannie stood staring ahead. She did not know what to say, or where to turn. Shriveling in place she uttered, "I only wanted to see you," and remained tacit thereafter, letting us take over what little conversation penetrated that brief, agonizing visit. Fannie left quietly with Harry, her heart heavy, her face dampened with tears.

I know Fannie would never have forgiven herself if she had not had the opportunity to gaze upon her younger sister's features once more—to be in her presence for those limited moments. The scene stays with me. I can still see the compassion scored across Fannie's face and, yet, the bitterness that wracked Minnie's ashen face.

Bloodlines are thick. Aunt Fannie supported the statement that had a way of entering our conversations, "There is nothing like family." These are the ties from your very own flesh and blood which cannot be erased, no less when hatred surges through that bond.

Minnie was buried surrounded by her husband, children, grandchildren, nieces, nephews and friends. And there, also, was Fannie, sobbing—Fannie, the last survivor of the four daughters whom Nathan and Ethel Shulitzky had brought to America more than fifty years ago, leaning on a cane.

"Why am I still alive?" she unremittingly questioned. To Aunt Fannie's way of thinking, "Longevity serves no real purpose." Fannie believed she had been merely existing for the past ten years or so, becoming more of a burden to herself as every movement coerced from her body became a major effort.

"There is no reason for me to live," she repeated, and rehashed the same words she had spoken before. "Your mother died and left you and Joe. Bella died and left Nora. Minnie died and left Millie. I have no children, no one who depends on me."

I made every effort to assure my sole aunt that her nieces and nephews cared for her well-being, that they were concerned about her. When we were young she gleaned admiration and respect from each of us. I think back to how Aunt Fannie observed each one of her nieces and nephews throughout our childhood, our teen years and our marriages, and glowed with us when our children were born. Her genuine fondness and interest never faltered despite the stormy conditions she may have encountered. Her frequent references to the "children-she-never-had" was evidence enough of her love for us all.

After Minnie's death, Harry and Paul continued to stay in contact with Fannie. The three in-laws shared their loneliness.

The men telephoned Fannie regularly and visited with her once a week. Even into their seventies they continued to drive to see her, and were happy to do small errands for their sister-in-law.

Not too long after Minnie's death, Paul's high blood pressure played havoc with his health. A heart seizure killed him in a matter of minutes. Paul's death perplexed Fannie and made her wonder even more as to why her turn had not yet come.

Chapter Seventeen

*M*illie and I cared for Aunt Fannie as best we could. Millie had grown closer to Aunt Fannie since her mother had died, and I had never severed ties with her. Although time was limited with our jobs during the weekdays, Millie and I made every effort to talk to our aunt as often as we could.

I visited with Aunt Fannie more often than usual, and we still spoke to each other every Sunday by telephone. It was Aunt Fannie who initiated the calls most of the time, but as the years passed she would forget what day of the week it was. When I did not hear from her at the usual time, I would dial her number. Upon hearing my voice, when she answered the phone, she apologized for not calling me. Aunt Fannie did not want me to spend my money to call her. She was upset, too, with her forgetfulness.

It was the mornings she did not answer the phone that I worried. She was either in the basement or, more often, asleep on a chair, deafened to the repeated rings. It was possible that Ben could have stopped by to take her to his house for the day, or she might have been at the synagogue for a special holiday celebration. Sometimes she called me ahead of time to let me know, and sometimes she forgot to tell me.

147

When there was no answer, I dialed her number again that same evening to make sure she was all right. How I worried when I got no answer until I called again the next day and heard her voice.

For the past year or so, I realized Aunt Fannie was becoming less and less self-sufficient. Millie, also, noticed Aunt Fannie's failing health, and it was she who insisted Fannie undergo an examination. My cousin made the appointment and drove Fannie to the doctor. An electrocardiogram was included in the examination. It was then that the physician discovered our aunt had an irregular heartbeat and put her on medication. Fannie took the pills according to the doctor's instructions, but in a short while she completely stopped them on her own. Keeping faith in the Divine Providence, allowing her convictions to guide her destiny, Fannie decided to let nature, alone, take its course. Life was exhausting her. Each step she took moved closer to losing her physical independence, and her memory was increasingly unreliable.

Fannie grappled with fear when the doctor, who saw her insecure walking and learned of her many falls, recommended she see an orthopedist. My aunt viewed herself in a wheelchair. The vision frightened her.

When the orthopedist completed his examination, he wrote a prescription for a brace to support the lame leg. He proposed the brace be attached to the new pair of shoes, but Fannie insisted that each one be a separate unit. The doctor also recommended that she progress to a walker instead of using the cane, which would balance the weight on both sides of her body equally. Fannie heard this recommendation as a warning. A chill ran through her body. Had she come closer to the fears she dreaded her entire adult life? She sensed the time would arrive when her legs would signal their transition to further deterioration, that nothing more could be done. Physically, she knew she was ready for the walker, and agreed to use it, but her mind could not accept the reality of a brace.

A shoe specialist arrived at the house to fit Fannie for a pair of shoes. The bill was exorbitant! But Fannie would sacrifice anything to stay out of the wheelchair, a thought that haunted her in the middle of the night. Nothing was too costly to maintain the independence she fought so hard to earn all of her life.

The metal brace was an onus. It was a hardship for Fannie to bend over and set it in place when she dressed in the morning. Once she managed to adjust it, the bulk of it weighed her leg. I found out that most of the time the truss lay in the bottom of the closet and Fannie, instead, put her trust in the walker alone.

Once more I turned to my tactics of persuasion in an effort to have Aunt Fannie just *consider* the possibility of living in a senior residence. Her protest rebuked me every inch of the way and, as always, it overrode my determination. Fannie savored her independence. Each time I broached the subject I spoke more persuasively than the time before, for now Fannie was in her eighties, and I found myself more worried about her with each passing day. But she was not ready to make a commitment.

"No," she would say. "I want to stay in the same house my mother died in. Why would I want to leave?"

149

Millie and I could think of no one who would look after our aunt with the same interest as a relative. Dolores had a job, and Fannie refused to have a housekeeper, even for a few hours two or three days a week. Millie was managing a business, Nora left Philadelphia to seek a place for herself in the many corners of the globe, and Rosalie was wrestling with her own health, which had worsened. Joe and his family had since moved to Kentucky. So for the most part. it was Millie and me, between our work schedules and during weekends, on whom the responsibility had fallen. If there was anything Aunt Fannie needed, I would see that her wish was fulfilled, if at all possible, and if there was an emergency Millie was immediately there for Aunt Fannie.

As often as I visited her, my dependency on the telephone increased, to hear my aunt's voice—to know that she was all right.

"How do you feel, Aunt Fannie?" I would question over the telephone.

"Like an old lady," came the quick reply. After hearing the same answer week after week, I soon changed my greeting, consequently changing the direction of the conversation as well. I spoke with an optimistic attitude and talked about our children, or an interesting show I had watched on television. On a few of the days I detected a gnawing dejection while she repeated the same question, "Why am I still living?" I was unable to give her an answer. At least she was up and around and managed at her routine, and she appeared alert.

The disciplined schedule Aunt Fannie adhered to was something she looked forward to each day. The cleaning and cooking, and the minimum of bookkeeping gave my aunt a purpose. But I was aware of how many times she fell walking from one room to another, and never could rid myself of the fear that one day she would land on the floor and remain there, unconscious, until someone found her similar to the episode when she fell in the basement years ago.

Compassionate neighbors showed a special affection for "Miss Fannie." They acted kindly toward her and the woman across the street still looked for the front door to open in the morning. Respect for Fannie was demonstrated with a barter arrangement between the man who lived next door and herself. The neighbor cut the small patch of grass in front of her house and trimmed the evergreens in exchange for use of the garage Fannie owned, located in the back alley of the house. It was an amicable agreement for each of them.

Because it was impossible to attend to the daily and weekly needs of my aunt, I found that not only my aunt, but I too, had became dependent on her wonderful neighbors. And when Jake entered the hospital for surgery, they made sure that her cabinets and refrigerator were replenished with foodstuffs from the supermarket.

Dolores, Fannie's tenant, revealed her kind temperament in the deeds she performed for her landlady whose strength was quickly failing. The young woman, knowing that Aunt Fannie was barely able to manage her housekeeping, and how many times she had fallen in an attempt to do the little work she wanted to do, took it upon herself to clean Fannie's apartment on weekends. Dolores straightened the apartment, vacuumed the rugs, and mopped the kitchen and bathroom floors with Fannie's approval. Dolores watered the plants that struggled to stay alive. The vines looked as fragile as Fannie who was trying to win the battle of life; at the same time both appeared to be overcome with the loss of will.

Though my aunt accepted her physical decline, her complaints were directed toward vision and memory. Her memory was such that often she would forget if she ate three meals on a given day. I feared she would forget to turn the stove burner off after warming her meals. She could no longer remember if she had talked to Harry, her *brother* as she now referred to him, on a particular day.

Harry, too, was concerned about his sister-in-law. He and my aunt spoke to each other every day without fail. He worried when he could not reach her, and she worried when he did not answer his telephone. Once a week, Harry traveled from his home in another part of the city to see Fannie. Approaching ninety years he was no longer allowed to drive for fear of causing an accident. Instead, he hailed a taxi to travel to her house. There they sat and talked for a while, and then he took a taxi home again.

One day when Fannie got up to see Harry to the door, he noticed that it was difficult for her to lift herself out of the brown chair that she favored. Beneath the cushion of the chair hid two thick telephone books. Harry who, at his advanced age, still walked with a spritely step, could not bear to watch Fannie's suffering. Without informing his sister-in-law, he ordered an automatic recliner to be delivered to her house. Harry was anxious to alleviate strain on Fannie's body when she maneuvered herself out of a chair.

152

It happened without much notice that Harry, who had been living alone in the high rise apartment since Minnie died, signed himself into a residential home for the elderly. Since, in his younger years, he had volunteered his time to the people living there, he was familiar with its environment. Now that he was experiencing a new lifestyle, Harry tried to convince Fannie that this kind of life would be better for her, too.

Harry knew when he was ready to make the move and looked forward to the convenience of its facilities. He was happy there; buses were available from the front of the door of the residence into Center City, and to the Jersey seashore, conveniences which Harry took advantage of. Being a gregarious person, he enjoyed people, a little jesting, and liked to hold conversations with strangers. He even did some harmless flirting with the women!

No longer did he have the worry of cooking and cleaning, even though he had taken care of these chores for himself. He cooked his own meals after Minnie died and told me how he measured five tablespoons of oatmeal in milk to heat his cereal every morning.

Perhaps it was Harry's influence, or maybe my unflagging suggestions, but Fannie, at last, was becoming more receptive to the idea of a senior residence.

"It can't be all that bad." she remarked, concluding her sentence with, "Bu-ut..." dividing the single-syllable word into two separate pitches, "It's not for me."

"Whenever you're ready, let me know," I told her. I had hoped that, in time, she would relent—if only to stop from hearing me harp on the subject. I discussed the feasibility of filing an application to one or two places I had previously mentioned, only to guarantee space should she change her mind. I made certain to stress that even if an application were filed under her name, she was under no obligation to enter the residence until she was certain the timing was right for her. I explained in more ways than one that the application could always be rescinded.

But fate has its way of playing tricks.

One mid-winter morning Aunt Fannie fell. It wasn't until a day or two after the accident that Dolores, the upstairs tenant, discovered Aunt Fannie was not acting her usual self. The woman was listless; she didn't seem to know where she was. And a bandage was attached to her head.

Alarmed at the condition in which she saw Aunt Fannie that fateful day in her apartment, Dolores telephoned my cousin Millie who lived a short driving distance from our aunt's house. She was glad to hear Millie's voice, to know that she was able to reach her. Distress straining her voice, Dolores gave my cousin a description of the state in which she found Aunt Fannie.

Millie grabbed her purse, left everything, and immediately got into the car. She was anxious to get to Fannie's house as soon as possible to find out what happened.

When she arrived, Millie questioned Aunt Fannie in an effort to glean some information, but quickly realized she was getting nowhere. The elderly woman could not remember anything, much less any of the details. In a state of fright, thinking that our aunt had suffered a stroke, Millie quickly called the doctor who previously had attended the woman. She arranged an appointment for that same day.

The doctor carefully examined Aunt Fannie, but could not determine what exactly had caused her confused condition. At the end of the examination, the doctor told Millie he did not find anything unusual, and sent the two of them on their way home. However, when Dolores saw my aunt the next day, it was apparent that Fannie's speech was incoherent—there was something decidedly wrong with the elderly woman. Her speech was rambling, her thoughts muddled, and there was a bandage on her head.

Again, Dolores dialed Millie's telephone and in minutes Millie appeared at the apartment. She tried to find out what happened but, once more, it was useless. The only thing Aunt Fannie could reason was that she had fallen. She could not tell what caused her to fall, or where she was headed.

Millie immediately called the doctor. He told her to bring Fannie to his office as soon as possible. This time during the examination, the physician noticed that one side of Fannie's face was reddened, and blisters were covering her skin. That was the clue to what had happened. He now could tell that Fannie had burned her face. But how? The doctor made arrangements for my aunt to enter the hospital as soon as a bed was available.

I was shocked when I learned that she had burned herself. Not knowing what to expect when I visited her at the hospital a few days after the accident, a wave of fright filled my body when I entered the room. I hardly recognized my aunt's sweet face. It was covered with white medication to soothe the burned skin, and her elbow was black and blue. She appeared so helpless that I thought the end was near.

She mumbled something to me about burning herself. Did she remember, I wondered, or had someone told her?

The doctors still could not ascertain whether Fannie had suffered a stroke, nor how she burned herself. Each day, however, she became more lucid and, gradually, there was a shift from a detached state of mind to coherency.

The recuperation period lingered. Aunt Fannie was able to get out of bed with help from the nurses, and it wasn't long after that she could amble slowly down the hospital corridor. In spite of her lame leg, the manner in which she shuffled her feet disturbed the attending physicians. They were convinced that my aunt's walking could be improved in order to experience fewer falls—she would have to learn to synchronize her feet with a walker. Fannie was disheartened that she had reached the stage of dependency, leaning over a steel apparatus to get herself from one end of a room to the other. However, she rationalized, if this is what the doctors recommended since her recent fall, they must know what is best for her, and yielded to their advice.

Physical therapy was indicated to build strength in her arms, as well as in her legs; the doctors suggested Fannie be admitted to the rehabilitation center just around the corner from the hospital. Here, Fannie was going to be taught to lift each foot higher to counteract the dragging of her feet.

When my aunt was well enough to be moved, Millie, who had taken time from her small business, drove Aunt Fannie from the hospital to the rehabilitation facility. Millie and I knew that our aunt was making a daily improvement and getting excellent care. But what about the future?

During rehabilitation Fannie underwent an intense program of learning to move each leg forward in synchronization with the walker, while her face continued to heal. She demonstrated a brighter outlook through her speech and her facial appearance. At last, a cheerful smile broke through a formerly depressed morale. Still, I sensed that her heart weighed heavily—and the lame leg heavier yet—for the leg that represented her burden for life was fitted with a new brace. The appliance, a lighter plastic one, reached her knee. New shoes were prescribed, a style different from what she had been used to—a soft rubber sole with a wedge. Fannie was learning how to walk all over again—to walk without stumbling.

Each morning for three weeks, my aunt marched back and forth the measured path. Though she was slated to stay for two weeks, the physicians decided an added week would be advantageous. Fannie would be more fully recovered before she was dismissed, and the extra stay would help reduce the risk of her body plunging to the floor through a misguided step as often as it had in the past.

At the end of the second week, Aunt Fannie asked a favor of me. "Would you bring me some sesame cookies the next time you come?" Like a child, she wanted sweets to placate her painful suffering. The request was a welcome sign that her spirits were mounting, a major step from her dwelling on her recent accident and her present physical condition.

I visited Aunt Fannie in the hospital and rehabilitation center often. But before driving to North Philadelphia, I stopped at her house on Malvern Avenue. My attention that day focused on the accumulation of envelopes that lay on the coffee table next to the withered plant. The mail was arranged in several separate high piles, dating back many years. I began to discover there was nothing my aunt threw away.

The time there gave me the chance to glance through bills—to separate the ones that were in need of payment—and lay them aside for Millie who wrote the checks and had Aunt Fannie sign from her hospital bed. There were no implications that our discerning aunt was going to relinquish authority over her accounts. She firmly specified that she was going to sign the checks as long as she was physically and mentally capable. Not even in her darkest moments did it ever cross her mind to surrender this privilege.

During the month of Aunt Fannie's hospitalization, Millie and I were on the telephone every night, for what seemed like hours, discussing possibilities and alternatives for Aunt Fannie's living arrangements. It was my cousin and I who were now forced to make decisions for Aunt Fannie. We were dedicated to making her as comfortable as possible for the final stretch of her life.

By this time, with the skin on her face healing, and the black and blue marks on her body fading, Fannie was in a mental state where she could not think rationally or logically all of the time. It was evident that my aunt would be unable to live by herself and yet, from past experience, she would be unhappy with a stranger to cook for her and help her bathe. Millie and I were in a dilemma.

A revelation suddenly hit me. Millie and I had become heirs to Bubba's message spoken to her daughters some thirty years before. The words spun in my head: "Take care of Fannie."

All the while, I kept in contact with Millie's sister Rosalie, and my brother Joe, informing them of every doctor's report and of the discussions between Millie and myself. While they sometimes offered suggestions, Rosalie and Joe respected our emotional ties, and our proximity to Aunt Fannie which gave us free rein to do whatever was in her best interest.

The soundest solution, it seemed, was to admit her into a senior residence, at least temporarily according to Fannie's way of thinking, as soon as she was released from the Rehabilitation Center.

It was a hollow victory when, under these critical circumstances, she nodded her head in agreement to leave her apartment and reside in a home. The time had arrived when there was no choice remaining but to place her where she could continue to live independently, yet have available the care she required. I think, also, that she came to the realization that she could no longer take care of herself. Aunt Fannie assumed that her affirmation was a consent to nothing more than a trial period. She presently abandoned any thought of deserting the dwelling that sheltered her memories in a cocoon-like existence for the past quarter of a century, while I knew her survival depended on the nostalgia that found its way in every breath of air she inhaled. For weeks, feelings of guilt surged through me and I trusted that, eventually, Aunt Fannie would come to accept this decision as a realistic solution at this time in her life.

Millie and I concluded that if a room were not available when she was to be discharged, the option was to permit Aunt

Fannie to live in her apartment until living quarters were obtainable. Under these conditions it would be imperative to hire a daytime housekeeper, contrary to our aunt's wishes.

After assessing a few homes, the York House seemed the best choice for Aunt Fannie. We realized it was located in North Philadelphia, a distance for both Millie and me to drive. However, each of us was willing to sacrifice driving time for the comfort of our aunt in anticipation of permanent residence there.

Meanwhile Dolores and her mother had come to see Fannie while she was undergoing therapy. When Dolores heard that "Miss Fannie" was moving to a senior residence, she tried to convince her to return to the apartment to live. Dolores prevailed upon our aunt to "come home." She told Fannie, "I and the neighbors will take good care of you."

"How kind," I thought, "that Dolores made such an offer." Regarding Aunt Fannie highly, her friends wanted to tend to her needs. But the risk was too great. The decision had already been made. I discouraged Dolores from persisting in her efforts to have Fannie back on Malvern Avenue. I told her the family would feel a greater sense of relief knowing our aunt was settled in a place where she would have twenty-four hour care.

The decision stood firm. Our purpose was confirmed, for in a few days we received word that space in the York House was available. Millie packed up Aunt Fannie immediately and drove her to her new home before any one of us had a chance to change our minds.

PART VI

YORK HOUSE

Chapter Eighteen

*I*t was a day in early spring of 1990. Most of the seats on the benches outside the building were occupied, a few elderly people enjoying the prematurely warm weather. Looking beyond the benches, the outer structure of the building appeared as a luxurious hotel to Aunt Fannie. Inside, a few residents were sitting in the lobby chatting with each other. Some of the women were playing cards, and one or two of the men sat huddled, their eyes closed. With Millie's assistance Fannie walked slowly to the office on the far side and registered for admittance.

Fannie's eyes grew as big as the expectations we held for her. She contemplated her new adventure ruefully. Millie and I hoped our aunt would acclimate, without difficulty, to a different way of life. We looked forward to the adjustment as an uncelebrated one. We knew Fannie had been used to being alone, secure in the surroundings of her own home where she enjoyed the company of friends and relatives who visited. Here, she was to have her own living quarters and eat lunch and dinner in the huge dining room on the first floor with the other residents. She would be served traditional food prepared in the manner to which she had been accustomed.

Fannie could stay in her room if she so chose, or sit in the lobby and talk to the other guests. Most importantly, she was also going to have health care, for the agreement stipulated that Fannie be situated on a floor with available round-the-clock nursing. Silence sheltered the loss of her independence as Aunt Fannie alighted the elevator. When it came to a stop, my aunt, Millie and the aide walked off the elevator, and turned the corner where a long hallway stretched ahead of them.

Fannie proceeded slowly, her legs supported by the walker on which she had learned to depend. Every once in a while Fannie stopped to catch her breath until, at last, the aide halted. They had come to the door on which the number of her new living quarters was attached. As the aide unlocked the wooden-hinged barrier that was to afford Fannie a semblance of privacy, and turned the handle, Fannie and Millie peeked inside to view the cozy atmosphere. They saw a spacious room, a smaller area than her former apartment, divided into several sections by partitions. The floor space granted Fannie fewer steps to walk to the kitchenette and to the bathroom.

Bright light shone through the huge glass windows, lending an airy quality to the rooms. Blinds above the window frames shaded the sun which appeared late in the day. The room looked barren, but Millie sensed that once a few of Aunt Fannie's possessions were added, our aunt was going to be happy here. We both took satisfaction in knowing Aunt Fannie was going to have many of the same comforts she was accustomed to on Malvern Avenue.

Millie employed a companion several hours each day for a few months until our aunt's health improved enough for her to be fairly self-sufficient. The hired woman was to make sure that Fannie ate her breakfast, and she was supposed to bathe my aunt. But sly Fannie knew the hour Irene was due. She awakened early to sneak into the bathroom and bathe before the woman arrived. Fannie did not want a stranger to wash her, no less see her undressed. I was annoyed at her premature claim to self-reliance. One of the reasons for engaging a companion was to ensure that someone be with her when she took such risks in the bathroom. I worried she would slip in the tub and fall.

When she rode up the elevator by herself for the first time, Aunt Fannie initially became disoriented and forgot the location of her room, and the room number. But this was not unexpected. Aware of the situation, I strung the key, imprinted with the room number, onto a long chain and hung it around her neck. Aunt Fannie did remember to wear the chain when she left her room for the day and, thereafter, was able to find her room without difficulty.

The elongated corridor to and from the elevator swallowed Fannie's frail body, seemingly an exertion for her to reach her destination. During visits, I watched my aunt struggle up and down the passage, the brace on her leg, a shrunken form bent over the walker. But Aunt Fannie still stood on her own two feet, protected by the four-pronged metal object. She concealed too well that the long trudge sapped her strength. It was pride that carried her.

Seats positioned opposite the elevators at the end of the corridor, across from the nurses' station, gave Fannie a chance to rest after the long walk from her room. Often she sat and waited until another woman or man got on the elevator, if only to allay a fear of riding to the main floor alone. She was in no hurry, for there was no place else for her to go, nor was anyone waiting to take her anywhere.

Generally, Aunt Fannie was complacent in her new environment. When she felt the desire for company and conversation she sat in the lobby from late morning until dinner talking to new-found friends. After dinner my aunt made her way upstairs to watch television and prepare for bed.

Millie and I decorated the prosaic room. My cousin brought the television from Malvern Street and placed it in a corner, convenient for easy viewing from the bed or a chair. She also brought a few pictures of relatives and arranged them across the bureau. I carried in the multi-colored afghan my mother had crocheted for her that lay on the sofa in her old apartment. The familiar articles symbolized a sense of security—a connection to the past, while at the same time, they enhanced the room. Radiating with warmth, the new apartment contradicted its simplicity.

The room was not the only thing Millie and I decorated. We knew of the scant clothing in Fannie's closet that took up little space, the few presentable dresses, outdated, and of dull colors. Some were threadbare and stained. We would have been embarrassed for our aunt to be seen in them. Back at the apartment we hastily stuffed the vintage clothing into trashbags and placed the bag in the outside trash can. At that moment we promised ourselves to purchase a new wardrobe for Fannie. We were going to dress her up.

To hide her self-designated "disgrace," Fannie insisted on dresses with long skirts. And now her consciousness was compounded by the brace she wore. Luckily, the wearing apparel that Millie, my wife, and I selected pleased our aunt. Fannie admired the bright colors we had chosen— flowered prints and stripes, unlike anything she had ever worn before. The humble woman was even more delighted that we took the time to shop for her.

I also bought a new apron. The flowered cover-up was designed to protect Fannie's modern outfits from the spots and stains that became apparent as her loss of coordination manifested itself. Despite my plan, her new clothing quickly became soiled. Although she wore the apron at mealtime with honor and dignity, it appeared not to fully shield her garments from the food that dropped onto her lap. Aunt Fannie had recently lost control of directing eating utensils into her mouth, so that food now rolled down onto her clothing.

Aunt Fannie always put on her favorite green dress to honor the Sabbath. She knew when Friday night arrived— linen cloths covered the tables in the dining room, and fresh flowers added a festive touch. On occasion my aunt attended religious services in the lower lobby, but more often she forgot.

Aunt Fannie's happiest moments were when she had visitors. She would sit in the lobby, majestically, on the oversize winged tapestry chair, waiting for her company. With failing eyesight my aunt attempted to read a newspaper, her head arched over in an effort to distinguish the fine print. Then when she lifted her eyes and caught sight of Jeannine and me walking toward her, a big grin instantly welcomed us. Bright red covered her lips, the colorful lipstick my aunt always wore on special occasions—the only make-up that ever touched her unblemished face. A necklace hugged her chest. Aunt Fannie "dressed up" for her company. With such words as, "It's the greatest of gifts you're giving me," Aunt Fannie expressed her appreciation each time we came to see her. As we sat and chatted I told her about my work. We talked about the children and the latest national news.

On a another visit Aunt Fannie introduced me to some of her friends, while we sat in a group and talked. Politely, one by one, the women left. When every one was gone, my aunt leaned over towards me and whispered, "The people around here are old." I suppressed my laughter of truth, yet gave away secret thoughts with a wide, mischievous smile. Did she not believe seeing people of our own age is a mirror image of ourselves? Human nature, I think, belies that admission.

The visits were filled with stories from the past, just as they were when I visited my aunt on Malvern Avenue. The tales were spun like the old 78 plastic records. Joyous moments, and sad moments, captured the time we spent together. There were moments full of nostalgia, and moments charged with regret.

In the middle of one Sabbath afternoon a woman sat at the piano in the corner of the lobby. Aunt Fannie was retelling a story in competition with the strains of Yiddish songs which filled the lobby. I listened, smiled and said, "Yes, I know, you have told me that once before."

I departed each time with ambivalent feelings. But I could never leave without hearing the story of how, with the encouragement of my parents, my aunt started her business.

My aunt's memories were blended with demure gratitude and reticent independence. And with each repetition I caught a twinkle in her eyes expressing a bit of self pride.

In her new residence, Aunt Fannie realized that Millie and I were as close to her as the telephone, and she dialed our numbers during the week when she had either a question or a problem. If neither of us answered the rings, Aunt Fannie, having grown accustomed to the answering machine, would leave a message on our tape. Her message, neverchanging—"It's Aunt Fannie"—received a quick response. By the time I returned her call she had forgotten the reason she phoned me. It made me happy, though, that my aunt found the telephone numbers in her small brown book and was now able to punch in the numbers on the new-style telephone. Still, technology was strange to her. It elated me, too, that although her physical capacities were deteriorating, her mental capacities remained with her.

It was comforting to know that my aunt was under good care and enjoyed the company of the other guests. She was not isolated as she once envisioned, having been unfamiliar with new, modern senior residences.

Yet she worried about the expense of living in a place as fine as this. Millie and I were certain that our aunt was financially capable of paying the costs required by these institutions from the years of thrift and the investments Aunt Fannie had made. Wasn't this what she had saved for all of her working years—to reap the comforts of old age? She needed the reassurance to dismiss the slightest possibility of ever having to become financially dependent on her nieces or nephews.

Unaccustomed to living in such a grand manner, she questioned, "How do I come to deserve such service?"

The most significant investment Fannie made was in herself.

One day I walked into the home after Aunt Fannie had her hair coiffed and her nails manicured sporting red nail polish, as bright as a fire engine. Millie was just leaving.

"Doesn't she look wonderful?" Millie remarked.

I saw a glow of contentment on Aunt Fannie's face I had seen rarely in the years before. Aunt Fannie's features reflected the same inner luster as her glistening, shampooed hair. Even some of the women in the lobby had complimented her on how well she looked.

As summer approached and departed, Aunt Fannie was aware she would live out the rest of her years in the residence. The inimitable question, "When am I going home?" dwindled with the passing of time.

Chapter Nineteen

*M*y aunt stayed in touch with her old friends. Some of them came to visit her at the York House, including Ben and Phyllis. Dolores traveled across the city, bringing her mother with her, to be with Fannie for only a short time. Frances called once in a while and chatted for a long period, and Harry continued to talk with Fannie every day, as he routinely had the last few years. Each of us discovered the best time of the day to reach Fannie—early morning, or after 7 o'clock in the evening.

Jeannine and I visited on one of those hot days of summer. Aunt Fannie was sitting in her favorite chair in the lobby, as usual, and greeted us when we walked in. Gripped in my hand was a bag containing some newly purchased clothes my wife and I had selected for her. Aunt Fannie was excited when we told her we had brought her some new wearing apparel. She wanted to try the outfits on immediately. She lumbered onto the elevator with Jeannine and me close behind. Aunt Fannie plodded at a steady, rhythmic pace with the weight of the leg brace, just as she had practiced at the rehabilitation center. I marveled at the strength and persistence of this indefatigable woman as she raised

169

the walker, lifted her "good" leg, then slid the other one the many steps it took to advance from the elevator to her room.

Reaching her quarters, she removed the key from around her neck and opened the door. Like a schoolgirl she was anxious to see if the skirts and blouses fit. In order to keep her balance, she sat in a chair and squirmed out of her clothes as I pulled the garments out of the bag. After trying on the outfits with their dangling price tags, Aunt Fannie's face beamed in approval with her brand new possessions.

My aunt favored skirts that fell below mid-calf in an effort to hide the brace. I believe Aunt Fannie only wore the appliance to appease Millie and me; she was not always sure when we were coming, and feared admonishment for not having it on. She became the child who submitted to guidance from a younger generation, although she found the brace cumbersome and would rather be without it. We, however, had only her welfare in mind.

The corridor to Fannie's room seemed to grow in distance each time I stepped in place beside her. We passed many doors before we reached the one with the familiar numbers tacked onto it. In fact, Millie inquired at the office about an available room closer to the elevator to shorten the walking distance for our aunt.

"No," Fannie insisted. "It is good for me to walk. I need the exercise."

Aunt Fannie never complained of the stretch, nor did I hear her talk of pain, except to mention the arthritis in her hands when she told me she could no longer sew by hand, or easily tear the bread for the birds. How proud I was that Aunt Fannie conceded to the distance from the elevator to

170

her room. It was an indication she was not ready to have things made a little easier for herself. She was not willing to give in yet, as long as she could walk up and down the halls leaning on the appliance.

Oh yes, she fell, once, that we knew of. The fall took place in front of the elevator. She told us how embarrassed she was. But she did not slip nearly as much as when she lived in the apartment on Malvern Avenue.

The calmness and pleasant attitude my aunt usually portrayed deceived me on one particular visit. I saw Aunt Fannie quite perturbed when I arrived. Before I even had a chance to ask if something was troubling her, she blurted, "Somebody took my dentures. They came in my room and stole them."

It was impossible to reason with her at the moment. All the same I made an attempt to calm her by asking, "Why would anyone want your dentures? They're of no use to anybody else. They were made only to fit your mouth." Then I added, "Perhaps you left them in the public bathroom when you removed them to clean your teeth." Denying her forgetfulness, Fannie refused to accept any other possibility of the loss.

The missing dentures were reported to the office. They were never found. I often wonder what did happen to them—they could have accidentally fallen into the trash basket. For a while Fannie was unable to chew solid foods, and she knew how unattractive her mouth looked with gaping holes and prominent gums. For the sake of her health, it was essential to have the plate replaced. Driving Aunt

171

Fannie to the dentist for fittings for a new bridge to be molded—and for successive adjustments—gave Millie an added responsibility.

With new dentures, my aunt ate in comfort again. It was then that she began to consume an excess of food and started to gain weight. The memories of hunger gnawed at her— food was too precious to waste—and she became obsessed with hoarding leftovers from lunch and dinner.

Following a meal, Aunt Fannie placed some of the leftover food in a yellow cotton print carry-all that was attached to the walker. The food remained in the bag until she reached her room and put it into the refrigerator. Often, as we said our good-byes, she groped inside the pouch for a few seconds and drew out a piece of fruit, such as a banana, placing it into my hand.

"Take this home," she coaxed. "It's too much for me to eat. They feed you too much here." After some cajoling, I hesitatingly accepted the offering.

I cannot forget the day I was ready to leave after sitting in the lobby talking with Aunt Fannie. Before I knew it, she reached into the yellow bag and pulled out a package enveloped in several paper napkins. Reality tricked my imagination as she lifted the grease-spotted wrappings and handed it to me. She uncovered the prize and what appeared, shrouded in white, stunned me. The piece of food I found myself gazing at was a small, oily smoked whitefish.

"Take it," she said. "Take it home with you."

The shock of a dead fish staring at me in the middle of the lobby was more than I had bargained for that day. I wanted to laugh and cry at the same time. I wanted to pity

Aunt Fannie for all the pangs of hunger and pain she had suffered as a child. This was one time I could not accept the graciousness of this grand lady.

"Thank you," I murmured. "You keep it. Put it in your refrigerator, you might get hungry later."

The face I held dear had grown fuller. Fannie had lost sight of her once healthy eating habits, unaware of the amount of weight she had gained. My aunt had added on a few pounds when Bubba cooked for her. But then, realizing she was getting heavier she made an effort to lose some of the weight she had gained.

Fannie kept a careful watch of the amount of food she ate when she cooked for herself. She did not eat between meals and although she was fond of ice cream, she kept none in the freezer. She denied herself the pleasure of eating the dessert because of its fat content, but would occasionally "indulge," as she described it, in a piece of pie or cake served at the home of a hostess. Once more, the width of her body had grown so much so that many of the new clothes no longer fit. With aging, she had since shrunk in height and now was extremely short, and because of the added weight walking was more of a struggle for the dauntless woman. And so it was to her advantage to lose approximately ten pounds. Afraid that she would add more pounds onto her once slender body, I tried to convince to her that she must not eat as much.

"It's not good for you," I warned.

"I can't waste the food," she rebuked.

"Instead of eating two pieces of bread," I suggested,

"eat one. It is better the leftover food be thrown away than you eat it and become too heavy. Weighing less will make it easier for you to walk."

Aunt Fannie heeded my advice and quickly changed her food habits. Vanity, too, played a small part in her decision to lose the excess weight, for even at her advanced age my aunt cared about her appearance. She started to leave more food on her plate, and the refrigerator in her room was not as filled as it once had been. Within a few weeks I could see a slight change in her face.

Chapter Twenty

I realized the first-floor apartment of Aunt Fannie's house on Malvern Street must not remain vacant. Millie and I held many discussions on this subject and concluded there was no advantage in holding onto the property. The house would have to go on the market for sale.

But the prodigious task of sorting through more of the paraphernalia accumulated over the years fell to me. Dear, frugal Aunt Fannie, who saved every scrap of paper, and every plastic and paper bag. When I picked them up, the transparent produce bags placed at the end of the sink in a neat pile disintegrated. I tossed the remnants into a black trash bag. The stockpile of food containers and lids, washed clean, lay orderly under the short counter. A brightly flowered apron hung on the hook near the stove. And the bandages on the table—I didn't know where to turn, where to start.

I remembered the many years I used to come to see my aunt. We both sat on the familiar sofa while she told me stories of the past, and years later, to my children. Beneath the end cushion on which she rested her body, lay the amassed piles of envelopes filled with receipts and bills, notices and letters requesting donations. That was her filing system, and the place I began my task.

Retrieving the papers from the folds of the furniture, I heaped them into my arms and set them on top of the sofa. I pulled each sheet from its envelope; most of the pages had no significance to the present. They could have long been destroyed. Poring through the assorted contribution solicitations, the few deposit slips and cancelled checks, time passed quickly. My aunt paid each bill and carefully recorded it. The collection of accumulated papers created a mound. I, once again, placed the refuse into a large plastic bag and carried it outside to the metal container into which I had already deposited many memories.

The books in the living room sat staring at me. I turned toward them and studied the collection, struck by their titles. I selected one book at a time, looked through it and returned it to its original place. Written on many of the inside covers were holiday greetings and birthday wishes. Those few hours were sufficient to launch my emotions— to feel the wretchedness of what further lay in store for me. Disbanding a home where fond memories exist is never easy. The feeling of a private emptiness pervaded where life once stirred. The void distressed me.

With the few books I wanted to keep and treasure tucked under my arm, I left. The rest would have to wait.

It took me almost two weeks to gather the courage to return once again. A queasy sensation filled my stomach each time I drove closer to the house. When I rummaged through her effects, it was as though I was invading Aunt Fannie's privacy. As close as we had been since I was born, as devoted we had been to each other in the last two decades, I felt it was not my right to search through her personal articles. On the other hand, everything in my aunt's life has been pretty evident. Aunt Fannie withheld nothing from the family.

Numbed by the obligation of destroying the past, my feet carried me into the bedroom. I saw the light streaming through the window and across the narrow bed neatly covered with its ivory-colored chenille spread. I observed the cherry cedar chest resting in the corner to the left of the door, and my eyes moved rapidly, scanning the open closet. I stood in awe questioning what I wanted to tackle first in this room. Quickly setting myself into action, I began to empty the drawers of the dressing table angled in the corner across the room. Opening the top drawer I saw that it was filled with bits of papers containing undecipherable numbers and addresses. Handkerchiefs, scarves and gloves, gifts from Minnie and Bella, were neatly folded in the middle drawer, and a multitude of aged sepia photographs, yellowed at the edges, occupied the whole space of the lower one. Working rapidly I was compelled to make hasty decisions—what could be salvaged, or what to deposit in another one of those black trash bags.

Since that didn't take too long I decided to investigate the cedar chest, too. I slowly raised the lid, the odor of camphor overpowering me. I gazed inside the piece of furniture in an effort to distinguish the items stored within. Aunt Fannie's gray Persian lamb coat lay on the top of the pile, obscuring the collection I later discovered beneath. Something pink and fuzzy showed through. My hand

177

reached for its softness, and I recognized it as the rug my wife and I had given Aunt Fannie one Chanukah. We gave it to her to replace the faded and tattered chenille rug which was still covering the blue ceramic tile floor in the bathroom. It had never been used. In my disappointment I let it drop gently to the floor.

Everything I touched reeked of the strong fumes of the camphor. After dropping each article to the floor, I tried to avoid breathing deeply, and continued my search.

What was this? My hands clutched a navy-colored bathing suit. I let out a howling, hearty laugh. Holding the garment up in front of me, I could see that it had sleeves and noticed the fabric was woolen. I wondered—it must have dated back to the '20's. The suit had been stored in this piece of wooden furniture for nearly sixty years at least. Styles have come a long way since then—no bare arms or thighs in this outfit! Neither were there moth holes; it was in perfect condition. Having been stored in the chest, the suit was protected from larvae for all of those years.

And here were the blue pajamas my cousin and I were searching for during Aunt Fannie's last hospital stay. Millie remembered she had given them to Aunt Fannie for one of her birthdays, and had looked everywhere for them. She was curious to know where they could have been. I left them on the bed so my cousin would see them. She'd be surprised, I knew.

I saw some white sheets stored below, and an envelope on the bottom containing a few silver dollars. Most of the things would be given away. Putting the items in piles on the floor, I left it for Millie to decide what she wanted to do with this collection.

I resolved to finish this room on my next trip. The closet would be the next thing for me to search through when I returned. It was time to go home. After closing up the house I walked to the car, the smell of moth deterrent lingering. The drive home seemed to take longer then usual while my mind and my emotions converged. Upon my arrival home I was anxious to get into the shower, but as I entered the house my wife, who was waiting for me and wondering how I made out, was there to greet me. My only response was my mumbling, "I hate this job, hate it, hate it, hate it...."

The closet looked empty without the hanging clothes. Worn shoes lay disorderly on the floor—the therapeutic shoes repaired to accommodate Fannie's lame leg. I tossed them into one of the bags I had brought with me and worked through the rest of the closet pulling hat boxes, square and round, down from the shelf above. I looked inside each one of them. The lids were covered with dust, and some of the boxes proved empty. Laying in one of the square cardboard boxes were a few hats that cloaked Aunt Fannie's head the days she sat in the synagogue and prayed—the same ones she had worn to her sisters' funerals. Each hat told a part of my aunt's history.

By the feel of its weight, I sensed no hats in the next box as I lifted it from the shelf, for it was much too light. Cautiously I lifted the lid, peering inside of it. A faded newspaper, folded in half, captured my attention. I opened the printed paper and absorbed the date. TUESDAY, SEPTEMBER 4, 1945 it read. Aunt Fannie was forty-two years old at the time. The headlines, "HISTORIC SCENES AS JAPAN FORMALLY SURRENDERED ABOARD USS MISSOURI," stared at me.

My mind was too occupied with the events of that momentous day, the day my brother would soon be coming home from his travails in the Far East, to give much thought to the small papers lining the bottom of that box.

Eventually I lifted the pieces of stationery out and slowly open the small sheets of paper. It was Aunt Fannie's handwriting I recognized scrawled across the pages. The heading across the top of the yellowed sheets read NATIONAL FIVE AND TEN CENT STORE, the date written along the top of each one. Grasping the papers tightly in my hand, I start to read the first page. I become aware that the blood was rushing to my head and my heart was pounding. Absorbed, I read further and found myself becoming emotionally distraught. These were letters of my aunt's diary that my eyes were focused upon.

A feeling of guilt overcame me. "I shouldn't be reading this; it's none of my business," The words and thoughts were too personal. And yet inquisitiveness pressed me on.

March 23, 1954

Yesterday I stabbed my heart again by inviting Leon to the theatre. Now my heart has seven wounds each wound deeper than the other[.] At the time of the stabbing takes place my heart is numb but after a few hours my heart begins to bleed and keeps on bleeding.

Right now I feel that my blood is leaving my heart. Why do I love him so much? What is in him that I want more than I ever wanted in my life?

The only answer I have is that I feel and know that
he is the only man I was looking for all my life.

Tears trickled from my eyes. With clouded vision I barely managed to finish the final paragraph. A wave of shock surged through my body. Questions leaped through my mind. Did anyone know at the time? Surely my grandmother must have found out about the infatuation because Leon's brother was at their house many times. Did Aunt Fannie ever tell my mother, her confidante? Her sisters would have scoffed, I know, if they knew Fannie was in love.

March 1, 1955

...maybe it will be better not to see him at all.
...late after noon [sic] by impulsive thoughts [I] might find him in the office but instead it was the book-keeper. Well as I did not have an order I just askt [sic] for Leon and if he is alright. ...because only to see him made me alive again.

May 23, 1955

He just left[.] I still see his face and hear his voice so near and yet thousands of miles away ...gosh how I wish to find a way to forget him!

June 30, 1955

About ll days ago I expected Leon but instead his brother came and said Leon will not come for quite a while because he is covering the cea [sic] shores...
But today I saw him across the street. In heavens [sic] name why does he not want to see me? Could it be he knows how much I love him...
Oh God I wish I would be dead.

July 20, 1955

It is six weeks since I saw Leon. And I can't stop crying for him. I cry in the nights and in the mornings and also through the days when the customers are not around.

September 2, 1955

Since June 6 Leon didn't call me. Today I was expecting him as he called two weeks ago on the phone that he will come today. The all (whole) day my heart was beating like Indian drums as I really made up my mind to ask him not to see me any more [sic].

...he will come in to say hello when he will be in the neighborhood and that we shall remain friends.

How many times, I wondered, did Aunt Fannie read and re-read her inscribed thoughts? How long did it take for her to get over her love for Leon? Did she ever?

Aunt Fannie was content with the simple things in life. And yet there was something very simple, and very special, she craved. Something that had no materialistic value, but an intangible possession that so many people have and take for granted. All my aunt wished for was someone to love, and to be loved in return.

I gathered my composure, straightened the place a bit, and left, my mind in a state of confusion. Arriving home, Jeannine immediately noticed the drained look on my face.

"How did it go today?" she asked, tension straining her voice.

"Look what I found," were the few words of my answer

as I pulled pieces of the diary from my pocket and handed them to her.

As she began to peruse the papers carrying the stale odor of age, my romantic wife gasped. I noticed tears rolling down her face. Through her sobs she blurted, "I just have to write that book."

Jeannine had talked to Aunt Fannie about writing the story of her life. When she had told my aunt that she wanted to write her biography, Aunt Fannie responded with a big grin, indicating a strong sense of satisfaction. She repeated the statement in her usual question form, "You want to write a book about me?" Her facial reaction was a response of how pleased she would be. The newly-discovered diary confirmed my wife's mission.

Chapter Twenty-one

*M*illie and I told Aunt Fannie that we were cleaning up her house with the intention of emptying its possessions. Then we intended to put the building on the market for sale. My aunt, in the meantime, never mentioned that she wanted to save anything, or that we might come across anything personal, or private. I am sure she had long forgotten the pages on which she recorded her most sacred secrets—secrets that must have been tucked away in the box for thirty-six years or more. They were probably casually placed inside the box in the similar manner she thought she was casually placed aside by the man to whom she would have given her heart.

After finding the pages of the diary, the visits with Aunt Fannie placed a strain on me. Did she ever dream that anyone would find these letters and feel the pathos of her unrequited love in the decades beyond?

From the moment I laid my eyes on the words of Aunt Fannie's romantic intoxication, I had come to view my aunt from a different perspective. A part of her life seemed to be missing—as though a piece of a puzzle were lost. I admired her wanting male companionship under the provision of true love. She did not want to marry under the guise of love—to live with someone who felt sorry for her or to someone who wanted a wife for a housekeeper and hope love would come afterward. It was puzzling that, in her chronicles, Fannie mentioned nothing about her "condition," for the consciousness of her deformity never left her.

But this was one rare time in my aunt's entire life that her crippled leg became secondary to a circumstance. Her lameness had always been a reason, not to be misconstrued as an *excuse*, upon which she based her rationalizations. How enthralled she must have been by the charm of this salesman to allow fantasies to rule over self-absorption with her handicap. Did the salesman spurn her *because* of it? Or did he plainly not possess the same feelings for Fannie as she held for him?

Fannie must have been extremely jealous of her sisters. How my aunt's life might have been different had she married! I think of how she must have yearned to have a family of her own more than anyone could ever imagine. I can remember the many times she said to me, "I never had children of my own, but you are my children." I felt a great devotion and an added responsibility to my beloved aunt. It was the way I had been brought up. She was a part of my family—my blood line. I could not abandon her. I felt a special affinity to her since the revelation of her memoirs.

It is not easy to watch a person age, to know the end of a life is closing in. But I saw her energy waning. I watched her inner struggle and detected her once-stalwart determination slipping away.

186

If Aunt Fannie were confined to that dreaded wheelchair, dependent upon strangers for all the things we who were younger and healthy took for granted, it would be sadder still. That was the very reliance our aunt strenuously strived to avoid. With all of her power she plotted a detour. Confinement in a wheelchair would cause Fannie to lose what will to live remained in her brittle bones. And, most certainly, sitting in a wheelchair would dissolve all the faith that had carried her through the years. I could not let that happen, for one of the things I had always loved about her was that, for all of her life, Aunt Fannie had been a fighter. Her religious faith, and the faith engendered within an inner spirit, had enhanced that will for all these years—and had seen her outlive her sisters, survive robbery and assault, and triumph over countless daily challenges and setbacks. She dealt herself the hand in the direction that faith allowed her—although she would never admit it. She knew from the moment she entered this country she was going to be self-sufficient, making her own way through life. Courage and a sense of purpose followed closely behind faith and determination.

The conversations continued, as usual, and the ultimate question followed each narrative. "I can't understand why I am still living. I'm an old lady." In response to her own disbelief, Aunt Fannie added, "It's a mystery to me."

I quickly reminded her of the answer the rabbi had offered after Bella's funeral: "Your time is not up yet," though a premonition I had made me sense the appointed time was drawing nearer and nearer. Aunt Fannie's overall physical condition remained the same. Her health did not appear to be deteriorating, and she seemed to be well cared for. Yet, each time I said "goodbye" I was stricken with the thought that this might be the last time I would see her alive.

When Millie and I discussed the sale of the house with Aunt Fannie, her only comment was, "What do I need it now for?" I interpreted the question as an acceptance of her new way of life, and an affirmation of happiness with the friends she had made. Her statement in the form of a question was also an acknowledgment of her helplessness, being unable to take care of herself, and a relinquishment of responsibility in maintaining the property. Practically everything in the residence is done for her. Her bed is made, her room is cleaned and her meals are prepared. She even commented to me that she did not think she could do housework or cook anymore.

Still, Aunt Fannie held within her heart the desire to see the house one more time before it was sold. My cousin and I concurred that that would not be a good idea. But when Fannie told Dolores of her longing, Dolores thought otherwise.

The young woman promised to ask a friend to drive Fannie to her old neighborhood in West Philadelphia. Dolores had hoped that if Fannie saw her old apartment once more, she would be strongly convinced this was where she belonged. The conflict between Dolores' aspiration, and the decision Millie and I made had to be resolved. It was up to me to discourage Aunt Fannie from returning to her former home. Aside from fear of what might lie ahead, I dreaded the thought of Dolores' responsibility of getting my aunt in and out of the car, and up the sloping steps into the house.

188

I was apprehensive that Fannie would fall, and I worried about the possible injuries she might sustain. Remembering when Fannie came to our house, not too long before, I had to lift the weight of her body as she walked up the one step to our front door. Now that Aunt Fannie had added extra weight to her small body, and was less sure of her footing, she was more difficult to guide.

Fortunately, I was successful in convincing my aunt not to take the chance. She agreed with the reasoning of her unsteady walking and graciously declined the generous offer. With that decision she dismissed the notion, forever, of seeing the house that carried memories of her dear family.

The sale of the house was advertised in the newspapers, but there were few inquiries. However, there was one man who evidenced a keen interest in the apartments, and we were told he placed a deposit with the realtor. To our disappointment he did not qualify for a bank loan.

While finalizing the few things that needed my attention back at the house, a neighbor approached me. Having missed seeing Aunt Fannie, or anyone coming to her apartment, the man made inquiry of his neighbor. He was taken aback to learn of her mishap, and that Aunt Fannie was permanently settled in the senior residence since her hospitalization. I then mentioned the house was for sale. The neighbor told me he had no idea we were trying to get rid of the property since there was no sign on the lawn. I knew that Millie had left some of the realtor's brochures on the table inside the apartment. I walked into the house to get him a few and immediately returned. Handing the papers to him. I also asked him to give the notices to anybody he thought might be interested in the purchase of the building.

It wasn't too long after that day that I received a call at my house from the agent.

"There is another bite on the property," he told me. The man, Mr. Washington, to whom I had spoken on my last visit, showed an interest in buying Aunt Fannie's house as an investment and wanted some detailed information about it. The realtor had already shown him the upstairs and downstairs apartments, and the potential buyer realized the work involved to renovate it—plastering and painting—and he was willing to take the risk.

I was excited that Mr. Washington was interested since I had seen how he modernized the house he had bought next door. Wicker furniture decorated the front porch, and fresh paint covered the railings. He replaced the wooden floor and railing of the back porch and built a small, attractive deck. I knew the house Aunt Fannie once lived in would sparkle with the same elegance when the work was finished.

A few days before the formal settlement arrived, it was necessary to clear the apartment of the furniture and the other things I had left. Millie was going to take care of selling the remaining articles, or else hire someone to pick them up and cart them away. I went back to the apartment for a final inspection, and my farewell visit.

Neither my cousin nor I dared to walk down to the dank basement. The lingering merchandise from the store—rolls of oilcloth, towels, handkerchiefs and a quantity of notions—since Fannie's retirement from the store some thirty years ago, rested in the darkness, untouched.

Whenever someone came to visit, Fannie would lumber

down the darkened steps, select an article or two, then climb up the stairs with the reserved merchandise in her arms. She would then ask her company if they had any use for the particular things she selected. Anxious for her unsold wares to be of use to others, she willingly gave the excess stock away. But the bulk of it remained, taking up space downstairs, and whatever was left was going to be sold with the building.

I called Dolores to tell her the house was on the market to be sold. It was the ethical thing to do. It would be unfair to spring such a surprise on her after the papers were signed. I wanted to personally thank her for her kindness toward Aunt Fannie, as well.

With the confirmation of a settlement date, I informed Aunt Fannie who had bought the property. When she heard Mr. Washington's name she reacted with surprise and great delight. My aunt was happy to know the person who was buying her building. Should it have been a stranger, I could have expected a display of remorse.

Chapter Twenty-Two

*T*he date of settlement had arrived. Since it was physically impossible for Fannie to attend the meeting, a form was waivered for me to legally sign my aunt's name. It was to have been only a business transaction. I had anticipated attending the legality of signatures unscathed by sentimentality. But when the day arrived and I started to write my name, an emotional separation took place. I felt a lump settle in my throat. It was as though an umbilical cord had been severed from our youthful years, and from the dreams and hopes of our grandparents who came with their daughters to seek a new life in America.

The sale of the house crushed the depths of my spirit. I recognized that my signature represented a completion— and inevitably, the end of a generation. The whole past lay before me. Too many memories lurked in that house through my many years of growing up, and I felt I had just lost a warm, familiar friend with all of the fond recollections the house contained. The years had passed too quickly. Both Millie and I cried the morning of the signing. It was Millie and I who remained closest to Aunt Fannie. We always regarded her with great esteem and came to love her more as a parent than an aunt, and especially so since each of our mothers had died.

Some of us live on memories alone, as did Aunt Fannie. Others leave memories behind and push forward to new and challenging things and ideas. Yet these impressions become a part of our lives, our experiences, the make-up of our character.

Once the papers were signed, there was no turning back. Yet Aunt Fannie was able to hold onto memories of the warmth and comfort, and the joys and sorrows of her family that filled her home here in America.

She had been secure on Malvern Avenue, unlike her home in Russia where the roof leaked and food was scarce—and despite all external transitions that challenged her during the forty-three years she lived in that house. Life had been good to Fannie, the so-called "black sheep" of the family. It was an accepted fact that Fannie sit in the shadow of her sisters and watch quietly as one watches acts of a play. There is no denying that life could have been a richer one for my aunt. Something was missing.

But she did not view it that way. She had been taught to make the best of what she had; she always appeared content. Yet she wished for so much more from her uphill struggle.

An invisible film protected Fannie's psyche. The layer shielded her from the persons most prone to be her censors—her sole critics, Minnie and Bella. My aunt never questioned why she, and not one of her sisters, was the one whose body was invaded by the virus that attacked her nerve cells. Never once, in her animosity, did she wish the disarming disability on either of them. She wanted only to be rid of the paralysis for a day, or for even a waking hour.

Fannie's leg was a constant reminder—always preying on her mind—a reminder that there was something different about her, that she was, in some way, abnormal.

Years ago, it was a *shonda*, a disgrace, if a woman did not marry. How Fannie admired married couples! Whether Fannie recognized if these couples were truly happy or not was another story. No one ever heard Fannie's innermost lamentations. One can only guess her thoughts concerning her views of singlehood. It was her mother's teachings and faith that allowed her to accept fate.

Even at the York House, where many residents walked with canes and walkers, the "X" that penetrated her clothing at Ellis Island reminded her that she was not the same as everyone else. She could never forget that. The only disabling threat throughout her life, in essence, was how she thought other people perceived her. Was it not ironic that the immigration official was going to reject her entrance to the country because of a physical affliction? A woman who deemed it her duty to live up to the demands of that singular person who had stamped her entry papers?

But Fannie did not accede to the victories of her survival by her own will and spirit since landing in America. Nor did she recognize the many lives she touched in her more than seventy years in this country. Nor all the people who endearingly attached the prefix "aunt" to her name. She made friends with whomever she met and wherever she went. Rarely addressed by any other name, as a very special woman my aunt stood apart from everyone else. Everyone knew her as "Aunt Fannie."

Behind her now were the years of hard work. The end of

195

her retirement brought a period of rest and relaxation. She had dared to risk the many obstacles that came her way. Still she succeeded in her financial goals, and succeeded in a personal promise—not to become a burden to anyone for her physical needs.

Aunt Fannie prayed for her destiny. Her prayers comprised of wishes, wishes that, at the end of her life, would find her standing on her own two feet. Her legs weakened, and her body lost its strength. The once alert mind became slow and many memories were purposely blotted out. Aunt Fannie had felt enough anguish in her lifetime.

"I hope to die in my sleep," Fannie expressed in the form of another prayer. For several years she repeated that request. She wanted to die peacefully and without suffering. Everything in her life was in order. She was prepared for the end of her journey.

And still spring arrived. Early flower blossoms appeared—a time of rejuvenation and hope.

I visited and talked about our garden and my roses. I told Aunt Fannie about my semester of teaching, about some of the young people with whom I worked. And I talked about the changing values in our society.

She, in turn, told me the year she was born and the year she came to this country. She could not remember how old she was, nor that it was 1991. Testing her mental acuity I checked her mathematics for her to determine her age. Finally arriving at the answer she smiled and remarked, "You know, I'm an old lady." And when I left she asked, "When will I see you again?"

The following Saturday Jeannine and I visited with Aunt Fannie again. Though she told me, "It has been a long time since you came to see me," I found it meaningless to explain that I was there only a week before. At once the small talk became predictable. My aunt rendered her customary story with the preface, "You know, if it weren't for your parents... "We talked and joked as I tried to keep her spirits afloat.

Jeannine and I said our good-byes and left. We walked through the doors into the bright sunshine with our private thoughts. Our eyes met in silent acknowledgment that our thinking was very much the same—we knew that Aunt Fannie would not be with us much longer.

EPILOGUE

A few days later—a Tuesday in May of 1991—our telephone rang at 10 o'clock in the morning. Jeannine answered the call and heard a woman's voice on the other end. Immediately she sensed the purpose of the message when the woman requested to speak with me.

I heard the woman's voice say, "I'm sorry to tell you that Fannie Shulitzky died in her sleep last night."

Aunt Fannie's time was up. Some wishes do come true, and her wish was granted. Faith in a spirit greater than her own had been reaffirmed.

Nieces and nephews, her brother-in-law Harry, and Phyllis and Ben gathered at the cemetery to bid their respects to our aunt. We had all grown to love Aunt Fannie. She had become someone special in each of our lives—and she told such wonderful stories.

The rabbi, who knew my aunt well, offered a final eulogy on this hot, cloudless day when suddenly, as if it had been rehearsed, a flock of birds appeared in the sky singing their farewell to this grand lady. At the end of services the mourners departed, slowly drifting away.

A few steps behind them, I turned my head back toward the grave and murmured, "Goodbye, little Faigele."

Jeannine W. Hamburg is the author of

Where is That Music Coming From?
A Path to Creativity